Watch Me
Daddy
The Cry of the Generations

MICHAEL TURNER

D1275102

ISBN: 978-1-890900-74-8

Library of Congress catalog card number: 2012936322

Printed in the United States of America

ENDORSEMENTS

"I am so glad that God moved Michael to write this book! It is a timely word for our world that will bring understanding, reconciliation and honor!"

Dr. Dale C. Bronner
Senior Pastor, Word of Faith
Family Worship Cathedral

"Michael Turner's book, *Watch Me Daddy*, speaks to all those who did not grow up with the treasure of a father's presence active in their lives. Michael nails it as he shares the heart of God through the pages of this timely book. God's desire is 'to restore the hearts of the fathers to their children and the hearts of the children to their fathers.' I highly recommend this book to anyone who genuinely desires success at the highest level of fatherhood."

Danny Chambers
Lead Pastor, Oasis Church

"Michael understands firsthand what it's like to grow up in a single household without a father. He also knows that the redeeming power of God can restore any relationship no matter how broken it has been. This book speaks to fathers, sons, daughters and single moms. It also brings healing to them all and inspires men on how to be great fathers. *Watch Me Daddy* is a book about healing and restoring the generations."

Chris Hodges
Senior Pastor, Church of the Highlands

"*Watch Me Daddy* is a wake-up call for this generation! Michael has done a tremendous job of combining the practical and spiritual principles of fathering a generation. This book truly is a game-changer and if applied, will help guarantee spiritual legacies in the lives of families for generations to come."

J. Ashley Jensen
Speaker and Author of *Getting Up*

"Having known Michael Turner since high school, I have observed him survive incredible odds to become an outstanding husband, father and leader. If you have faced challenges in life, relationally or otherwise, this book is a must read."

Rob Jones
Senior Pastor, Church of the Harvest
International

"The need for a father's approval is present within each of us and provides the motivation for much of our lives. With great personal understanding and wisdom, Michael Turner shares insightful truths about our earthly fathers and our heavenly Father. As a father myself, I know the many lessons taught in this book have lifetime value for both our present families and the generations to follow."

Dr. Dave Martin
America's #1 Christian Success Coach
Author of *The 12 Traits of the Greats*

DEDICATION

I dedicate this book to my three amazing children, Michael Jr., Presley and Madelyn. I treasure every moment I get with you. You helped inspire this message and I want you to remember that daddy is watching you always. I want you to take this treasure of generational blessing God has given to you to go further, faster in your lives and for those coming after you! Go to your destiny....

CONTENTS

Foreword

THIS WONDERFUL BOOK that my friend, Michael Turner, has penned is really about the importance of key relationships. To a large extent, the evolution of social media has created a conundrum and paradox for us. While it has promised greater connectivity, it has delivered artificial relationships and personal isolation. Genuine relationships foster real community and build bridges instead of walls.

A beloved spiritual father of mine, Ed Cole, taught me that relationships are the essence of life, and communication is the basis of relationship. Relationships connect us to destiny. They keep us from being an island unto ourselves. They are like bridges. Some are long and broad and take us over vast bodies of water. Some are short and narrow and only take us over a ravine or a marshy area. Likewise, different relationships have varied time assignments in our lives. Some are only for a season. Some are for a specific reason, and when that is accomplished, the relationship dissipates. Yet other relationships are for a lifetime!

The relationship of a father is one such lifetime relationship. A teacher teaches what he knows, but a father imparts who he is. God is the preeminent Father, our heavenly Father. No other relationship is ever designed to substitute for our relationship with our heavenly Father!

But God has given us fathers in the faith, like Father Abraham. In fact, God's promise to Abraham was that in Abraham, all the families of the earth would be blessed (Genesis 12:3). Ironically, the Old English word "family" literally means "father's house." This is not to diminish the importance of mothers or even single mothers that exist, but to emphasize the significance of what a father provides to the household.

A father is a progenitor of the generations. God chose Abraham, not merely because he was a good man, but because He knew Abraham would pass on to his generations the things that God spoke to him (Genesis 18:18,19). God curses one-generational thinking. The fullness of God can only be seen and experienced through the generations. That's why God became known as the God of Abraham, Isaac and Jacob.

God only blesses us when we are connected to His ultimate purpose. That's why I am so glad that God moved Michael to write this book! It is a timely word for our world that will bring understanding, reconciliation and honor! I believe this book is a response to the closing prophetic words of the Old Testament:

"Behold, I will send you Elijah the prophet before the coming of the great and dreadful day of the Lord. And he will turn the hearts of the fathers to the children, and the hearts of the children to their fathers, lest I come and strike the earth with a curse" (Malachi 4:5,6 NKJV).

Now let the turning begin!

Dr. Dale C. Bronner
Founding Pastor and Author
Word of Faith Family Worship Cathedral

Acknowledgements

First, I want to thank Father God for always watching me and never giving up on me. Thank You for restoring me to allow generational blessings to flow to my children for a thousand generations.

I want to thank my beautiful bride and best friend Charla for inspiring me to believe in myself. Thank you for encouraging me to write and share my story.

I also want to thank my mother for always believing in me. Thank you for your faithful love in raising me through it all and for helping me find faith in Christ!

I would like to thank Dr. Henry Jones and Dr. Dale C. Bronner for fathering me into manhood. Thank you both for opening your arms to embrace me and validate me.

Thanks to all my dads, Eddie Turner, Randy Adams and Charles Poole, for what you have added to my life as well. I love you all.

Introduction

IN THE FALL of every year, my wife and I, along with our three children, take a family trip to Hilton Head, South Carolina. In 2006, when my children were ages six, four and three, we were all playing on the playground when I first noticed something profound. I am learning to grow in the art of multitasking as a father of three young children trying to give attention to each child all at once. I was a little winded in the dusk of evening when I noticed they were always asking me to watch them as they performed on the playground. They wanted me to watch every act and movement they made on the monkey bars, slide and swings. They didn't care if I couldn't look at all three at the same time. One would call out, then another, and frustration started to set in.

It was then when I heard God speak to my heart very calmly. He said, "Just watch." It hit me that they had been wired by God with the need to know that I was watching. They needed to know that I was interested in their abilities and achievements. They simply wanted to make me proud. It brought them such a sense of accomplishment to know that I was watching them cross new boundaries of growth. It was as if it was their gift to me. They were crying out, "Watch me Daddy."

As I reflected back on my own life, I realized it was something that was missing deep within my own soul. Looking back I noticed that my whole life, that's what was missing. I wanted to make my father proud of my life. I realized that being a grown man, a father with children of my own, how intense the desire is to have a father looking at your life watching you, affirming you, coaching you and cheering for you. I understood in that moment, and as I pondered my failures and short-comings from the past, what I was truly longing for was my dad to be in my life, watching me. I believe Solomon heard from God when he was inspired by the Holy Spirit to write the following words:

Children's children are the crown of old men; and the glory of children are their fathers.

Proverbs 17:6 ASV

Children are one of life's greatest blessings. Ancient Hebrews desired to be surrounded by a large band of grandchildren rather than having a literal crown. A large number of children guaranteed the stability of the family, while at the same time, children eagerly boast about their fathers if they have reason to. Here is a powerful incentive for a father to live honorably, so that his children should have reason to be proud of him.

The glory of children is their father. This literally means adornment or an ornament of pride. We may not want to admit it at times, but I believe it's true. We want to make our fathers proud of us, and we want to be proud of our fathers. One very proud child may be known to boast by saying, "My daddy can whip your daddy." I am sure Solomon, being the son of King David, could identify with this as he was constantly referring to his father when writing Proverbs. It's evident that Solomon's glory was his dad, King David.

My Story

In my own life, I recall the void I had in my life from the father who was in and out of my life. I can remember 1975 very vividly being five years old. My dad, with suitcase in hand, got into his car and drove off down the street. I don't recall any conversations, but somehow in my heart I knew Daddy was leaving and not coming back. I can remember running out the door into the street as fast as my little legs would take me in pursuit of Dad, crying as I ran calling out to him. I don't know if he saw me or not, but he didn't stop. As I stated before, in my very young mind my heart somehow knew he was leaving my mom, and even at that age I could perceive that. After watching him drive away until I couldn't see his car any more, I ran back home all the way up to my room crying until I hit the bed.

Being in the middle of a divorce is hard for any child or person for that matter. I remember despising seeing my mom or dad with another person in a relationship. Perhaps I was extremely vocal about my displeasure of it and made life for their potential dates hard. In short, I did not like them and they knew it!

It was only a year or two after that my parents remarried and things were good for a while, but that would not last either. I do have some good memories of my dad in that short season of life when my dad actually coached my baseball team. It meant so much to me that my dad was the head coach of my team. The joy didn't last long as soon afterward I was awakened in the middle of the night with my bedspread wrapped around me, and I was put into the front seat of the car with my mom as she went out looking for my father who hadn't come home from work. Mom's suspicion was typically accurate, as she would find my dad in the wrong place with the wrong people.

As usual he was gone again and it was Mom and me doing life together without Dad – first days of school, Halloween, Thanksgiving, Christmas, birthday parties and sports. My mom was great. She would be team mom and be as involved as she could in everything I did. Those are the last memories I have of my father's active role in my life.

A few years later my father moved on, eventually remarried to begin another life with another family. I was around twelve when that all went down. So as I was entering into puberty, the deck was already stacked against me by not having an active father present in my life to help shape me and direct me through my most challenging years ever. I did well for at least another year; I still played football, had good grades and was active in church.

When I was thirteen I was introduced to marijuana for the first time and was seeking joy from the pain of rejection that I didn't even know existed in my life. I am not saying I didn't make a bad choice. I was curious and I wanted to belong so I did it.

About a year later I began a relationship in which I would become sexually active and for the first time I felt like I had identity because I had a relationship and I was fitting in with the popular crowd. Little did I know it was the beginning of a deadly downward spiral that would only get worse in every way.

When I was sixteen I quit playing football and my grades were barely passing. I was very possessive of my girlfriend from my extreme insecurity so I found myself fighting a lot. I was at war with my girlfriend, my mom, my teachers, my peers and myself and really with God.

When I was seventeen I experimented with harder drugs for the first time with some friends of mine who were in college. This opened the door for heavy use of alcohol, tobacco and yet even heavier drugs.

Later that same year I found out that I didn't have enough credits to graduate and was going to have to watch my classmates that I had been going to school with since elementary school participate in a ceremony I was disqualified from. Over that summer in 1988, as if that wasn't enough to make me realize the pit that I was in, my longtime high school girlfriend broke up with me to date another guy she eventually married. Who could blame her? I was a quitter and a loser at the time. What was supposed to have been a year in my life that I would never forget had become the worst year of my life that I tried to forget by drowning myself deeper into alcohol and drugs.

So there I was at eighteen with no father, no diploma, no direction and no hope. I tried to go out and make something of myself. I went from job to job with a bad attitude and a bad work ethic. No man ever cared enough to successfully discipline me and teach me the tough lessons I needed as a stubborn teen about money and commitments.

I eventually started getting into clubs at nineteen, which exposed me to more drugs and more promiscuity. I seemed to somehow temporarily lose the pain of my life while intoxicated, trying to escape into a world that was purely deceptive as well as destructive.

One December night I was caught in the parking lot of a nightclub consuming an illegal substance by an undercover officer. I spent the night in jail and began to make promises to God that I wouldn't keep. I got off with a first offender's warning where I had to be on probation and do community service. However, I once again slipped back into a life of drugs and alcohol.

Four years later I went to a concert on a Friday night that ended up in a three-day binge where I took a large amount of drugs that led me to the emergency room at a local hospital. While lying there staring at what seemed to be certain death, I really began to evaluate where my life was and where it needed to go. It was at that moment that I felt as if this could be my last day on earth. I knew that I would face the eternal God whom I was not ready to meet. I then cried out to God and decided that I was not ready to die. I wanted to live. I was given medication and released from the hospital the next day. I was twenty-four years old with a dead-end job, a lot of habits (none good) and very little hope.

THE FATHER'S HOUSE

I decided I was going to go to church and see if I could find hope there. I walked in and I felt shame and fear. I felt as if I had let a perfect, holy God down, and I had, but I didn't realize how merciful and loving He was either. I decided that I was going to commit to Jesus Christ and I was going to commit to church. It wasn't easy as I felt I didn't fit in and I didn't know a lot about the Bible either. I decided that in January of 1995. I entered that church a hurting, addicted, rejected young man. I had been lost. I knew that my father wasn't watching me, and it didn't seem to matter. I didn't have anyone to make proud, and nothing to live for really. I believe every child longs to make their father proud.

It wasn't long after being in the Father's house that I discovered my heavenly Father's love. I discovered that He was watching me the whole time. Even from the time I was a little boy when I was going through all the pain of my parents' divorce and running down the street after my father, God was watching over me. He never stopped loving me even when I was living a life of reproach and rebellion. I discovered that when I should have been judged, I found mercy. I deserved hell and He gave me heaven. He gave me grace for my guilt and forgiveness for my failures. It was in His presence and in His house that I decided I was going to live for Him and make Him proud by living a life of honor. I decided that I was going all out and not holding back. I had found my true Father and my identity as a son. That affirmation from Him brought wholeness and a stability in my life that caused me to have hope that I could be something as a man.

God didn't stop there, He placed me under a great man with integrity who was a good father and coached me into manhood, a spiritual father who would speak life into me and affirm my call and gifts in the Lord. He surrounded me with men of faith who began to validate me, causing me to believe that God could do something big in my life if I would let Him.

In the fall of 1995, I started Bible College to pursue more knowledge of this loving God who was reaching out to me. I connected in a local church, serving anywhere I could as often as I could. I began to share the amazing life-changing message of God's grace with anyone in close proximity to me. It was only a year later when I was invited to serve on staff of that church as a youth pastor. I was blown away at how God was giving me the opportunity to speak to a generation who were at the very station in life as teens where I was when I drifted or rather walked away from God. I served for four years before being invited to serve as my pastor's associate for another two years before God would call us to start a new work on the southern crescent of Atlanta, Georgia. We launched out to start Turning Point Church in January of 2003.

Now more than seventeen years later as a validated son, I am a husband, a father of three beautiful children and the pastor of a thriving young church. I owe it all to my heavenly Father, my mother and all the men who so selflessly poured into my life. Although my earthly father did the best he knew how, and may have mishandled me, my heavenly Father never left me or stopped watching over me through every step of my journey. He never intended for my story to end in the agony of defeat but in overcoming victory. I know that this same loving God of the Bible, God the Father, doesn't want your story to end in pain either, my friend.

I started looking back at my life and I noticed as I looked up my family tree that my parents were divorced and their parents were divorced too. This is my story so far and it has inspired me to write this book to all of the sons and daughters who are hurting in some way. I am also writing this book to fathers everywhere to encourage them to be their best and to let them know that it's never too late to start actively watching your children.

I want to speak to single moms too. I was raised by a mom who loved God, introduced me to church and to Jesus Christ! If you are a worried mom because your children don't have a father or one who is presently involved, you need to know there is hope for you. You can have protection and faith for your children to rise up to do something significant in life, fulfilling their potential. God has a legacy for you, your children and your children's children. You can be the X factor, the game changer.

It is my sincere prayer that this book will bring hope, healing and restoration to the millions in our nation who have father wounds in their soul. I know God is on the move to heal those who are broken-hearted and who have been bruised inwardly. God has not forgotten you nor has He forsaken you, but He is taking you by the hand and walking with you to your place of victory!

CHAPTER 1

The Cry

SINCE THE DAWN of time, our need for being fathered is deep. From the time we are children until we are grown, we desire the presence of a father in our lives. However, each night in our country, approximately 40 percent of American children will go to sleep in homes where their fathers do not live. We are living in a country of fatherlessness, a country that was founded by strong fathers. Our land is filled with dads who have fallen from decades of generational wounds that have caused the foundation of our culture to continue to erode. The result is that there are far less committed fathers in our culture than ever before in our history as a nation.

Unlike earlier periods of time when fathers were perhaps absent because of war, our cultural loss is more than physical and it affects every home. The future of our country lies in the balance concerning this matter of fatherlessness. The lack of good fathering in our society directly affects us in a number of ways. For instance, it affects who we are as males and females, what type of society we will become, and even more importantly, the way we understand and relate to God.

We live in a time when our culture is more fatherless than ever. For most who have had fathers present in their lives, even those relationships have often been more negative than positive. But the need to be fathered is an essential, fundamental need of the heart.

I once read where singer and songwriter Bob Carlisle was quoted in regard to his hit ballad, "Butterfly Kisses," a song that speaks about the love between a father and his daughter. Bob Carlisle once said, "I get a lot of mail from young girls who try to get me to marry their moms. That used to be a real chuckle because it's so cute, but then I realized they didn't want a romance for mom; they wanted the father who is in that song, and that just kills me."

The desire expressed by those little girls is the same longing we have for our fathers and especially Father God. Our hearts long to be fathered in this world because God the Father wired us that way. There are no perfect fathers in this world. God alone is the perfect Father.

I believe that every child has an intense desire, a cry if you will, to know that their father is near, watching, and that he is extremely interested in what they are becoming. We so desperately want a father to watch us, to "look at me, Dad. I am doing my best to make you proud! I want to make you proud. Your approval means so much to me. I love to hear you brag on me and see your face light up when I do something significant. Watch me Daddy."

From the time that Adam was walking in the cool of the day with God to the time of Abraham, Isaac and Jacob; through the time Moses was gleaning from his father-in-law Jethro on leadership lessons, even until the birth of Jesus, scripture records that He had an earthly father figure in Joseph who would love Him, father Him and even train Him in the ways of carpentry.

Jesus spent much time with His earthly father Joseph, and Jesus eventually took on his trade of carpentry to perhaps run the family business until He began His ministry at thirty years of age. From scriptures we can also see that Jesus longed to be in the presence of God the Father too. Often, He would separate Himself to be alone with Him in prayer.

When He came to the end of His life, we see Jesus crying out in the Garden of Gethsemane before His betrayal, all the way to the end of His life on earth while on the cross, finally committing His spirit into the Father's hands. Jesus was living for the glory of the His Father. He was living to honor the Father and quite possibly could have been the force I am speaking of when it comes to us knowing that we have a father watching our lives.

It seems as if there is a secret source of power released from our hearts that highly motivates every son and daughter to live to the fullest when they have this sense that a Father is watching them blossom into what God destined them to become. For example, I read a couple of stories that back up what I am trying to say. The first is about a young major league pitcher you may have never heard of, but he had his day in the spotlight. I believe it was due to the fact that he was playing for an audience of one, Dad. His name was Jonathan Sanchez, a pitcher for the San Francisco Giants. Sanchez had recently been demoted to the bull pen, but he was given a chance to start after Randy Johnson went on the disabled list from injuring his shoulder. Sanchez's father had never seen him pitch in the majors before because he lived in Puerto Rico. This night of destiny was linked to his father's presence.

With his father in the stands, Sanchez pitched the first no-hitter in the Giants' organization since 1976. That is how rare a no-hitter is. In fact, the only reason it wasn't perfect is because of an error by the third baseman. Guess who was one of the first to congratulate him after the game? His father. He was in the dugout embracing his son to punctuate the fact that he was there and he watched every pitch. "This is **the first time** he [dad] has seen me pitch," Sanchez said. "**I was pumped** that he was here **watching** the game."

Wow! Did you notice the secret sauce for Jonathan was his dad being in the stands for the first time? Why this time? He had already been cut as a starter three weeks prior from the not so stellar performances previously as a starter. What was the difference? Or rather, who was the difference? Dad, that's who.

When Dad is watching, we dig deeper, play harder, dream bigger and go higher than we ever could without him. When Dad believes in us, it gives us greater courage to believe in ourselves. Jonathan made history that night, and Dad was there watching all the way. Way to go, Dad!

Another story that I read which caught my eye was about renowned investor Warren Buffett who talked about his father's involvement in his life and how it affected him for the good. He said, "There is no power like unconditional love… Every parent out there who can extend that… it's going to make for a better human being."

Think about that. One man noting the impact of his father as the main reason for who he is today. This billionaire is leading an initiative to rally the world's billionaires to give half of all they own to charity.

This is just a couple of great stories of lives that were impacted by the presence and love of a father watching them. We yearn to make our dads proud, and when we have a father or father figure actively involved in our lives at any age, we seem to be better.

WHAT IS GOD DOING?

Malachi 4:5,6 says, *"Look, I am sending you the prophet Elijah before the great and dreadful day of the Lord arrives. His preaching will turn the hearts of fathers to their children, and the hearts of children to their fathers. Otherwise I will come and strike the land with a curse."*

I realize that many scholars believe that this was fulfilled in John the Baptist, while others believe it has yet to happen literally before the return of Christ to earth. I want to look at it in another light. I thought about the spirit of Elijah, meaning a prophetic voice indicating something that the Spirit of God is calling for. God is speaking clearly to us in various ways to show us that He is coming soon, and a part of that promise is to restore fathers and children.

This book is simply one of the vehicles God is using to encourage us to expect His healing hand to restore what has been stolen by the enemy of our souls, Satan. The years that were taken from those of us afflicted in this father fallout, God is going to replace with more and then some as we turn to Him, trusting Him at His Word. There is a movement taking place in our land to move the hearts of fathers and children to be reconnected so that we can prepare to receive our King of kings and Lord of lords just as He promised to do before the coming of the day of the Lord.

It is my humble honor to be just a small part of that through this book and the messages I share with others. It would take an entire chapter to share with you all I have seen on numerous themes in movies, books, television shows and with the people I have encountered, including my own life. In fact, God is speaking loudly through the most popular sanctuary in America, "The Movie Theatres." I can't even list all the films today with father themes: Nemo, The Wild, Everybody's Fine, Warrior, Real Steal, Abduction, The Tooth Fairy, Mr.

Popper's Penguins … and especially the latest film called "Courageous." God is speaking through the channels America tunes in to most. My heart echoes that same message. In fact, I challenge you to look through this lens and be amazed at how many movies today carry some type of father theme within the plot. I believe it's because God is working in the hearts, minds and lives of people in our culture. He has not forgotten His promise to work on the hearts of fathers and children so that this land can be blessed once again.

I believe God is calling fathers to be healed and to turn their hearts toward their children. As you can see, Dad, from this scripture, it's the father's heart that turns first, which in turn causes the child's heart to turn. We are losing the hearts of the children of our country to destructive appetites and habits. I know they simply need their father's touch to bring their wandering hearts back to the Father's house.

This is one of the main reasons for writing this book. I believe God wants to speak through it, and my prayer is that through it the hearts of fathers and children can be mended! I sense that God is working in our land and in our hearts to turn this around for our good and for His glory!

As stated earlier, it doesn't take long to look around our culture to see how deep the father wound goes, since it is being expressed through various art forms in our culture – movies, music, books, sports and even ministry.

One night while flipping channels, I happened to see a special on CBS about the life story and success of hip-hop artist, Lil Wayne. While being interviewed by Katie Couric, Wayne described why he goes by the name of "Wayne" instead of his given name, Dwayne. Carter explained, "I dropped the D because I'm a junior. My father is living, but he's not in my life and he's never been in my life. So I don't want to be Dwayne. I'd rather be Wayne." Couric then asked Wayne if his father knew of this and Wayne replied with a smile, "He knows now."

Wayne went on to say that he received a phone call from his hero, Jay Z. I thought it was interesting what he said in their short phone conversation. Wayne recalled picking up the phone and the only words that Jay Z said were, "*I see you.* I see you." I believe he was affirming this young man longing for validation by saying, "I am watching you." Somehow Lil Wayne understood what he meant.

As I looked into Jay's history, I read that his father had abandoned him at the age of twelve. In some way Jay Z was and is a father figure, perhaps to that community of hip-hop artists. I think its meaning could be interpreted in many ways, but I also believe it was the affirmation of a father figure that he received. I believe that Jay perhaps had this revelation too that we need to know that a father is watching us grow into a man who is reaching his full potential. We all need that in some way from someone we see as a father.

Not only has the lack of good fathering shown up in hip-hop, but in other forms of music as well. I remember reading about the life of lead singer for the band Creed, Scott Stapp. I noticed that a lot of his inspiration for his music was driven by strife between he and his stepfather. He never knew his biological father. I personally loved the lyrics of Stapp as I could somehow sense the place he was writing from in some strange way. Imagine my surprise when I read about his challenges with his father growing up. My point is that there are millions who are creative and through their art expressions their "cry" is being heard.

During my teen years back in the 1980's, I was drawn to various types of music for many reasons, but I was also drawn into music that was somewhat violent in nature. Many of the lyrics were full of anger, rage and revenge. Today these tones and messages are not only in hard driving metal songs, but in hip-hop and pop as well. Once I found myself wondering why it seems that in the decades since then, the music and lyrics seem to get harder, angrier and outlandish.

When I was a youth pastor in the late 90's, I remember coming across this scripture in Ephesians, chapter 6, verse 4. It had a word to children to obey, and then it speaks directly to fathers: *"Fathers, do not provoke your children to anger by the way you treat them. Rather, bring them up with the discipline and instruction that comes from the Lord."*

A lack of godly fathering will cause children to grow up angry. I think that is why we see so much of it in popular music today. I really believe children are crying out to their fathers in anger, and inwardly they are saying, "Why did you do this to me? Why don't you love me and watch me by being interested in my life? Why don't I matter to you? Am I not worth it? Am I not worth fighting for?"

I believe the decline in youth accomplishments and the rise of negative statistics are directly linked to this missing ingredient so vital to the outlook, motivation and outcome every person has. I believe deep within our hearts there is a cry, one that must be heard and answered, if we are to truly be all that we were created to be. This is what I refer to as "the cry of the generations."

The gaze and presence of fathers is so deeply needed in our culture today. Sons and daughters who have grown up without a father or who have a father wound can be consumed with selfish ambitions and what feels good, trying to fill the void of validation they never received from a loving father. In the midst of this pursuit, men and women can overlook the need within their own children's souls that cries out for the attention and affirmation of a father. I have good news for you: God hears you and so do I.

My inspiration for this book is to speak out for all of us who did not grow up with the treasure of a father's presence active in our lives and for all of those who may have been emotionally fatherless. To the sons and daughters of our country who are now men and women, fathers and mothers, grandfathers and grandmothers, God has heard your cries and is fulfilling His promise to turn this thing around just like He said He would.

I also believe this book can help those of you who have had the blessing of a father in your life to remember how important you are in this world. And to single moms as well who are going it alone to know that you can make a difference in the lives of the generations all around you. This next generation is of the utmost importance.

CHAPTER 2

The Evidence Speaks

I LOVE AMERICA and I love being an American. I thank God for the faith and integrity of our Founding Fathers and for being born in a great country where people use that title, "Founding Fathers" with such honor. Because of their extraordinary success in laying a foundation for this great country, would they believe that America resembles what it does today, with over half of America's children being fatherless?

Research clearly identifies the effects that fatherlessness is producing in our culture today. It is unbelievable when you start to dig into some of the facts concerning children who are growing up with an active father in their life. Growing up in the 1980's, I didn't realize that one of the things that would mark my generation was divorce and single-parent households. My parents divorced for the first time when I was five and then again when I was twelve. I practically grew up without a father in my home and really not in my life except for the occasional calls and visits to his house.

Over the last couple of decades, many books and stories about fatherlessness in America have been written. My goal for this chapter is to simply get us to see what is the root of our generational and cultural problems in America. I want to focus on the root to remind us how much we need the presence of a father watching our lives.

Zig Ziglar said, "We will never solve the crime problem in America until we solve the problem of fathers not loving and training their sons."

I once attended a Leadership Conference where football coaching great Bobby Bowden was speaking. He said he was once asked by the media, "Why do you think the children are worse today than when you first started coaching many years ago?" He responded, "It's not the children who are different; it's the lack of good parenting and really fathering," as he recalled that most of his athletes were raised by single moms.

Prior to the 1960's the American family and fathers were very strong. History tells us that it was in the 60's when the push back came from our culture towards the family as well as towards God. It was in the 60's that the Ten Commandments were taken out of schools, and crime went up by some 2000 percent the very next year. I am not pointing the finger at any one generation as my parents grew up in that time, but I am just noting when a lot of this fallout began. George Washington University sociologist Amitai Etzioni said, "The 60's attacked all authority and institutions, including families and fathers."

President Bill Clinton, who was born without knowing his father, said this: "Fatherhood is rapidly becoming the number one social policy issue in America," and "the single biggest social problem in our society may be the growing absence of fathers from their children's homes, because it contributes to so many other social problems."

As a nation, the negative effects of fatherlessness have seemingly gotten worse with every generation. In fact, some psychologists have pinpointed that there is a large group of young people in their twenties (from age twenty to thirty) who are in what is being coined as a "lost decade." They are marked by extreme hopelessness, which manifests in many areas of their lives. They don't stay in long relationships or commit to jobs. They are giving up because they are hopeless. Could it be because they are crying out for a father? Could it be that the realities in their world are merely a cry from their souls, saying, "Someone, be my dad"?

I tend to believe this is one of the reasons for the great response of young adults voting in the last election, because someone promised them hope. Is it a coincidence that it was a man who knew about fatherlessness all too well who was a prime candidate – a candidate who, now president, knew what over half of this generation has felt growing up without an active father in their lives? I think he knows exactly what it was like and the hopelessness it can breed in one's life.

What happens to a country when over half its sons and daughters grow up without a father's voice and touch in their lives? What happens when Daddy is not watching? I think that the following data should give us accurate information for a reality check!

According to 72.2 percent of the U.S. population, fatherlessness is the most significant family or social problem facing America.[1]

Fatherlessness is linked to higher rates of poverty, failure in school, teen pregnancy, substance abuse, violent crime, depression and ultimately a loss of hope.

Some fathering advocates say that almost every social ill faced by America's children is related to fatherlessness. Six of the social ills are noted here. As supported by the data on the next page, children from fatherless homes are more likely to be poor, become involved in drug and alcohol abuse, drop out of school and suffer from health and emotional problems. Boys are more likely to become involved in crime, and girls are more likely to become pregnant as teens.

1. **Poverty**

   Children in father-absent homes are five times more likely to be poor. In 1996, young children living with unmarried mothers were five times as likely to be poor and ten times as likely to be extremely poor.[2]

2. **Drug and Alcohol Abuse**

   The U.S. Department of Health and Human Services states, "Fatherless children are at a dramatically greater risk of drug and alcohol abuse."[3] Children growing up in single-parent households are at a significantly increased risk for drug abuse as teenagers.

3. **Physical and Emotional Health**

   Unmarried mothers are less likely to obtain prenatal care and are more likely to have a low birth weight baby. Researchers find that these negative effects persist even when they take into account factors, such as parental education that often distinguishes single parents from two-parent families. A study on nearly 6,000 children found that children from single-parent homes had more physical and mental health problems than children who lived with two married parents. Additionally, boys in single-parent homes were found to have more illnesses than girls in single-parent homes. Children in single-parent families are two to three times as likely as children in two-parent families to have emotional and behavioral problems. Three out of four teenage suicides occur in households where a parent has been absent.[4]

4. **Educational Achievement**

   In studies involving over 25,000 children using nationally representative data sets, children who lived with only one parent had lower grade point averages, lower college aspirations, poor attendance records and higher dropout rates than students who lived with both parents. Fatherless children are twice as likely to drop out of school. School children from divorced families are absent more, are more anxious, hostile and withdrawn, and are less popular with their peers than those from intact families.[5]

5. Crime

Children in single-parent families are more likely to be in trouble with the law than their peers who grow up with two parents. In a study using a national probability sample of 1,636 young men and women, it was found that older boys and girls from female headed households are more likely to commit criminal acts than their peers who lived with two parents.

A study in the state of Washington using statewide data found an increased likelihood that children born out of wedlock would become a juvenile offender. Compared to their peers born to married parents, children born out of wedlock were:

- 1.7 times more likely to become an offender and 2.1 times more likely to become a chronic offender if male.

- 1.8 times more likely to become an offender and 2.8 times more likely to become a chronic offender if female.

- 10 times more likely to become a chronic juvenile offender if male and born to an unmarried teen mother.

- 85% of juvenile delinquents came from fatherless homes.

- 60% of America's rapists came from fatherless homes.

- 72% of adolescent murderers grew up without a father.

- 70% of long-term prison inmates are fatherless.

Having a father at home is no guarantee that a youngster won't commit a crime, but it appears to be an excellent form of prevention.[6]

6. Sexual Activity and Teen Pregnancy

Adolescent females between the ages of fifteen and nineteen years, reared in homes without fathers, are significantly more likely to engage in premarital sex than adolescent females reared in homes with both a mother and a father.

A survey of 720 teenage girls found:

- 97% of the girls said that having parents they could talk to could help reduce teen pregnancy.
- 93% said having loving parents reduced the risk.
- 76% said that their fathers were very or somewhat influential on their decision to have sex.

Children in single parent families are more likely to get pregnant as teenagers than their peers who grow up with two parents.

A white teenage girl from an advantaged background is five times more likely to become a teen mother if she grows up in a single-mother household than if she grows up in a household with both biological parents.[7]

I understand that even with two parents, there are no guarantees, but one thing is seen through these stats: It certainly does reduce risk significantly when there is a loving father active in his child's life. You must understand the lens that I see through when looking at these studies is one that can verify these stats as very true. As I discovered these tendencies of fatherless children, I could say without a doubt that they are evidences of my past. I say that because I experienced every one of them with the exception of physical illness. I was heavily involved in sports from age six. As I look at all these statistics, I can say "yes" to all of them.

Let's run through them again to see if you or anyone you know, love and care about exudes these qualities in their life today.

1. (*Poverty*) - When I did work, it was for very low income living at the poverty level.

2. (*Drug and Alcohol Abuse*) - I was first exposed to drugs at thirteen and I was drinking every weekend by age fifteen. That led to me drinking almost daily in my early twenties.

3. (*Physical and Emotional Health*) - I was easily angered, destructive, abusive and fearful. I could not keep a healthy relationship with my mother or girlfriend, and I couldn't relate to my teachers, coaches or employers in a healthy manner.

4. (*Educational Achievement*) - As a young child, educational achievement was something I felt inspired by, pretty much an A student in elementary school. By the time I reached seventh grade, my desire rapidly declined and I did the bare minimum to get by to the next grade until it caught up with me. I didn't have enough credits to graduate in my senior year so I dropped out of school at eighteen.

5. (*Crime*) - Obviously, being involved with drugs and alcohol led to an arrest at age nineteen with possession charges. There was only one instance where I was actually caught in the act.

6. (*Sexually Active and Teen Pregnancy*) - Yes, this too. I was sexually active as a teen and my girlfriend became pregnant which led to an abortion.

I was one messed-up Georgia boy going down fast. I was wasted and I was wasting time. I think it's clear to see that our country, which was founded by strong Christian fathers, is no longer being reproduced by and led by fathers of the same spirit and vision – not to take any credit away from the phenomenal women (*thank you, Mama!!*) who have and still play a vital role in making America great. Their roles are vital to the full development of children as well. However, based on the statistics, we have more of a fatherless problem than we do a motherless one. Even from these numbers it is plain to see that the absence of effective fathering is and has been very detrimental to our society.

I cannot see how America can continue to be great with half of its children fatherless. If our culture continues on its current path, things will likely be much worse in all these areas for our grandchildren and great grandchildren.

The main contributor to fatherlessness in our country has been divorce. With the high rate of divorce in our country, nearly one out of two marriages ending in divorce, it is easy to see why fatherlessness is on the rise. This fact isn't meant to condemn those who have experienced failed marriages. My parents divorced when I was five, then remarried when I was six, only to go through a sequence of separations again and again until I was twelve when a final divorce transpired.

It was the norm for Dad to be in the family one month and out the next. As a child I didn't know what was really happening because I thought that's just the way it was. I had no idea the negative reverb it was sending out that didn't show up until my mid teens and early twenties. It is amazing how messed up I was, and at the time I thought I was doing all right, which was far from the truth. As I look at these statistics, how damaging it can be in today's world without a loving, active father in a young person's life. It seems to be getting tougher for each generation, so the need for the rise and restoration of loving, godly fathers is now more than ever.

A Theory as Why the Fatherless Are Bent Towards Substance Abuse

Laughter is a gift from God. It is something God gives us that releases endorphins into our physical bodies and benefits us in so many ways. Genuine laughter has power to heal us in many ways.

I was on a flight back from Dallas, Texas, when, in the seat across the aisle was a little boy who was probably three or four years old. His mother said he was going to see his daddy, and the boy couldn't contain himself as he shouted out, "I can't wait to see my daddy!" Something else I noticed was how much he was laughing and enjoying himself.

My children love to laugh. In fact, we all do. I believe laughter is something our Father in heaven gives to us at birth, and as we grow up in a home with two loving parents, somehow our souls are just happier. I thought about how in my own life laughter was turned to sorrow when my parents divorced, and laughter seemed to have left my home. Maybe as a young man without a loving father active in my life, I began to look for fabricated laughter through the use of drugs and alcohol.

The picture projected from many movies was that these things made you happy and filled your life with laughter. I wonder if this is why those who delve into a life filled with these destructive habits also have a father wound in their life? I found out that no amount of drugs and alcohol could ever fill that void or that hole in my soul. Only the genuine, unconditional love of my heavenly Father could. He gave me the oil of joy for mourning and turned my weeping into dancing. I believe that He wants to restore genuine laughter to all who have lost the pure joy of laughter that comes from the Father's presence in our lives. In His presence is fullness of joy!

My joy for the little boy waiting to see his daddy turned to sorrow for him. After arriving at our gate, we were waiting to stand up in the plane as we all do before finally exiting the plane into the terminal. I overheard the little boy ask his mommy why she and his daddy couldn't be married anymore. I can't imagine having to answer that question. My heart went out to her as well as to the little boy. She could only say, "Because your daddy and I want to be happy so you can grow up happy."

I found myself praying for the mother, father and that precious little boy. I will be honest, I found myself holding back the tears as we walked off that plane. I could only think about the potential pain that little boy had in front of him. For me, that pain was very real as it is for every one of us who have had to go through the pain of having our parents separate and divorce.

My prayer was that somehow that family could be restored and put back together again. I know God is able to heal and restore broken people and families when we turn to Him with all of our hearts. Perhaps only in eternity will I ever know if God answered my prayer. Unfortunately, that is the story in so many people's lives today. I thought about how beneath that little boy's laughter was uncertainty and confusion over what was going on. I am choosing to believe that God heard my plea, and in His amazing grace He went into action on the little boy's behalf.

More Than Money and Fame

Jason Davis, an heir to the billionaire Marvin Davis, became addicted to many things, heroin being the most destructive substance he consumed. I was drawn to his story as he came from wealth and had a father around but who was not involved in his life. As I discovered the root cause of his addiction, I was moved to tears when in a session with Dr. Drew Pinski, he said he was raised by security guards and wanted to please his dad. He had a hole in his soul that was plain to see when he would talk about his father. To this day he feels like he's not good enough. He said, "I just want a dad to turn to and talk to." Isn't it amazing that even with billions of dollars around you and in your future, it still wasn't enough?

All the money in the world can never replace the love and presence of a father. Never!

WE ARE NOT WITHOUT HOPE

Father God is on the move, and there is a movement that is focusing on encouraging and equipping fathers to be who God created them to be. Many times we focus too much on who we used to be and not enough time focusing on who we were created to be.

There is a sound going out in the land through great organizations like the National Center for Fathering, Championship Fathering and Carey Casey. Other great movements are All Pro Dad with Coach Tony Dungy, not to mention books because Father God has heard the cries and prayers of the fatherless. He will hear and defend their cause. He is a Father to the fatherless. He is turning the hearts of the fathers to their children and the hearts of children to their fathers! His plans for America are good, to give us a hope and a future. He is answering prayers and fulfilling His promise according to what He spoke through Malachi.

A few years ago God put it on my heart to send one of our pastors out to find out what the greatest need in our community was. Without a doubt, the most common thread we discovered was the desire for teens who needed mentors. God opened a door for us at a local high school that was actually an alternative school for teens who had been removed from their primary schools. We call it Dream Builders. Our goal is to help students realize that God has a dream for their life, and that He has placed every gift and talent they need inside of them to accomplish that dream – a dream that, if lived out, will make them most satisfied and God most glorified.

We spend ten weeks for an hour-and-a-half connecting with students by eating, playing games, speaking and small group discussion. The students are required to attend at least two Saturday morning community outreaches where they help construct homes for the elderly and the needy. Thanks to our good friends at the Fuller Center of Henry County.

After completing three semesters, we found it to be no surprise that around 95 percent of all these students have an absent father who had abandoned them, some they have never known and some who were incarcerated. Though the semesters start out with a lot of attitudes, kids acting hard and trying to be cool by not participating, without fail we have seen the majority of even the hardest kids blossom into new seasons of their young lives. Students who were not smiling or respecting those around them were transformed into young people who have hope and a sense of purpose in life. They began to realize that God loves them and they have a purpose.

From the evidence in this chapter, we need to acknowledge that we have some really clear proof that many of our problems, as President Clinton put it, go back to the fatherlessness in our country. The bad news is that this is real and it's all over the place. It's in the homes, the government, the schools, the marketplace and even the church.

The good news is, now that we have identified the root causes, we can know where to begin to pray and take action in joining God as He has already begun the wonderful work of healing and restoration in our land that will help bridge the gap between fathers and their children. This, in turn, will strengthen us individually, as families, as communities and a nation that can be great again.

Will you take this journey with me to see God turn the hearts of fathers to their children and children to their fathers so that His blessing can continue to flow to our generation and the generations to come?

CHAPTER 3

Identity Theft

IDENTITY THEFT IS one of the number one crimes today in the U.S. In 2008 there were over 10 million victims reported in the U.S. alone. Every day innocent people are preyed upon and violated by thieves who trespass by stealing their personal information. These perpetrators then apply for fake identification so they can enjoy luxuries at the expense of someone else. These thieves can steal, kill and destroy a person's credibility and cripple their identity, thus hindering one's future way of life.

In the same way, the Bible says in John 10:10 that there is a thief who comes to steal, kill and destroy our lives as well. This thief, however, is out for more than just material goods. He wants to destroy more than our credit score or borrowing power. He wants to destroy our very souls. He preys not only on individuals, but on entire generations. He wants to steal generational blessings, destroy families and kill relationships, especially the ones we have with our fathers.

I believe that it is largely due to the fact that fathers are so instrumental in the development of our identity. Our identity plays a crucial role in the way that we see ourselves, the way we see others and the way we see our world. Our identity affects how we think as well as how we approach life. Everyone needs to know who they are and whose they are.

In fact, identity is crucial to everything or everyone who wants to fulfill its potential and purpose. Every successful business has an identity. Nike has "the Swoosh" and Michael Jordan. Microsoft has windows and Bill Gates. Macintosh has Apple and the late Steve Jobs. Football teams have their brands and mascots. Churches have mission statements and logos. Even gangs have an identity with specific colors and hand signs. In the same way, identity is extremely significant to every individual who wants to fulfill their potential and purpose.

The Heart of a Son is Shaped in the Breath of a Father

Fathers are very instrumental in the development of our identity. Fathers have the power to affirm us and validate us. I truly believe that every child needs a father.

The greatest need a child has is a father looking them in the eyes, and saying, "You are my child." Every son and daughter needs to be validated. Even Jesus Christ was publicly validated by the Father. This was prior to Him stepping into His ministry here on earth.

In Matthew 3:17 we see God the Father validating His Son, *"And a voice from heaven said, 'This is my Son, whom I love; with him I am well pleased'"* (NIV). When God the Father affirmed Jesus as a Son, He was reinforcing Jesus' identity so that He would be secure in His manhood.

In Luke 4:3 when Jesus was being tempted by Satan in the wilderness, he tried to get Jesus to question His identity by saying, *"If you are the Son of God...."* I love the fact that Jesus never responded. Satan, who is filled with pride, was tempting Jesus to question His own identity. Have you ever noticed that Satan started out every statement with, "If you are the Son of God." He was trying to get Jesus to question His identity as a Son. Pride was first noted in the heart of Satan, which caused his fall from heaven.

Pride at its core is satanic and from scripture we know that God resists the proud, but gives grace to the humble. Satan still uses this tactic today, but because of the father gap in our culture, it works for him very well because many people do not know who they are or whose they are.

Jesus simply responded with scripture because Jesus was secure in His identity. He knew who He was and whose He was. This truth brought Him great security. I believe this is largely due to the voice of the Father He heard at His baptism that empowered the humanity side of Jesus, saying, **"You are My Son** and in You I am well pleased." Jesus knew who He was and whose He was; therefore, He couldn't be a victim of Identity theft.

If we are going to overcome the identity issue, we are going to have to be affirmed by our heavenly Father as a son or daughter of the most High God. I also believe it is extremely important to have that expressed in a tangible way through our earthly fathers who can be biological by marriage or spiritual fathers.

Not having had the affirmation and touch of a father in my life caused me to be extremely insecure. I was always trying to get laughs in class, causing me to get in trouble often. It caused me to not be able to trust because of fear of rejection or abandonment. It caused me to be critical of others, and I had a negative outlook on everything in life really. Insecurity caused my heart to be full of pride. In fact, I believe that the root of pride is insecurity. It's my theory that Satan attacks all of us in this manner, especially those who are parents or potential parents so they will have a distorted view of who they are to affect their parenting or lack thereof. If he can do that, he can distort the children's view of who they are.

It is primarily the father who is to affirm and validate us and launch us into our purpose as the Father did Jesus. If our fathers can't or don't do this, then we can fall prey to identity theft which gives us insecurity that is the root of pride. It has been called "the ride of pride." Pride keeps us from God's grace, which is really what this is all about, keeping us from our heavenly Father's reconciliation of grace through Jesus Christ. God wants to bring your balance to a zero. That is what "to reconcile" means.

Today many people struggle with insecurity and identity. I truly believe one of the core factors is because they have never been affirmed by a father. They have never sensed the Father's love and His whisper in their hearts, saying, "I love you. You are mine. I chose you, I believe in you." They have never had a man pursue them or look them in the eye, and say, "I am proud of what you are becoming. I love you, I believe in you."

I didn't have this affirmation until I was a man who was seeking God with all my heart. Then it wasn't until a year or so after that when I was in ministry before I had a spiritual father lay his hands on me, look me in the eyes, tell me of my value and tell me what great plans God had for me. That's when I can distinctly remember becoming a son. Then God began to heal me in so many ways that I didn't even know I needed. He was settling my search for identity, freeing me from my great insecurity.

We can't overcome insecurity by just being more confident in ourselves. Don't get me wrong. We need to be confident in ourselves, but not really in ourselves. We need to be confident in who we are in Jesus Christ.

Identity issues have crippled our society. We live in a culture where children are growing up without a godly father to help define their identity. When good fathers, godly fathers, are removed, it tends to distort our identity and people find themselves looking to other sources in an attempt to gain an identity, even if it is the wrong one. In gangs, for instance, young boys and girls will turn to a dangerous, violent life, risking their own, just to try and grasp at something with which to identify. These brave young people are willing to take a brutal beating just for a chance to be embraced by the idea of a family or a father who feeds their need to belong. Hearing from these young people who turned to gang life or left it, they clearly express identity as a root issue for joining a gang in the first place. One recent poll said that 64 percent of those who joined a gang did so to find some sense of identity.

Poser?

Could it be that many of these young men and women are simply posing to gain acceptance? They are not living up to their potential nor do they see their divine design. They are posing a lot like Jacob posed as Esau his brother to get his father's blessing. Isaac loved Esau more than Jacob and what a profound effect it had on him. Jacob was willing to put on goat's skin, his brother's clothes and trick his father, just to be blessed and validated by his father. His name actually means a trickster and a deceiver. Jacob tricked his dad and his brother by posing. Jacob posed to get his father's blessing.

Young men and women who are posing, trying to be someone they are not, do so to gain an identity with success in entertainment, sports, fame and possessions. It may not be a gang that one jumps head first into to try and find identity. It may be fame or fortune. Sometimes even in ministry, men and women believe that if they can just have a large, successful ministry, it would establish their identity. For those who are doing this or are trying to, please know that these things and accomplishments can never fulfill you.

As one who has been in ministry for fifteen years, being on staff as a pastor for six years and as a lead pastor over the last nine years, I discovered early on this truth that attaining to the so-called success of having a large ministry would somehow validate my worth in this world until I learned that even after you achieve your goals, only the affirmation of knowing who you are in Jesus Christ as a son or daughter really fulfills you. It's the identity that we need to know that we are sons and daughters of the all-time greatest Dad in the universe .... Father God ... Daddy!

It is paramount that we talk about this and take action to bring this message of God the Father if we are to see the generations healed. We have a nation of men creating babies without considering the reality that every decision they make, good or bad, is going to affect their generations as well as future generations. Because they don't understand who they are and whose they are, the curse is in the land.

Children who have been abandoned or have never been affirmed are stumbling into adulthood, struggling to become what God wants them to become as adults. Thus, they are destined to repeat the same cycle they themselves are caught in, which is precisely why I am writing this book. God wants to change that. God wants to be a Father to the fatherless. We all need that, especially the generations who have been affected by it. The stats from the previous chapter on the results of fatherlessness confirm this truth. But God is on the move and He is turning hearts so that He can reverse the curse by releasing the generational blessings once again.

How do I know that we need to settle the identity issue? I was one of those kids. I was trying to find my identity in sports, music and then eventually in girls as well as the wrong crowd. Those crowds introduced me to drugs and alcohol. I was trying to win the approval of the crowd. I can remember looking to the world and trying to connect with different groups of people. I was trying to identify with rockers, trying to connect in nightclubs, dancing and endless partying still to no avail. I was wasted and I was wasting time.

Every boy needs to be crowned by a father to rule as king in manhood. Every daughter needs to be swept off her feet by a king to escort her into womanhood, guard her heart and perhaps one day walk her down the aisle to give blessing upon her marriage to the man God has chosen for her.

Maybe you are like me and you were raised in a single mother's home without a father. Or maybe, you are like millions of others where the father was in your house but not in your life. Years were spent searching for affection, affirmation and acceptance, wandering into a barren land without purpose.

After Jesus was affirmed and validated by His Father, He went into the wilderness to be tempted by the devil. He didn't give in to evil. He was anchored in the validation of His Father's voice. Every child needs to be validated and affirmed by their father, to know that wherever they are going in life or whatever they are becoming, they need to know their father is proud of them. It enables them to not give in to evil or go down wrong paths. It gives them the strength to do the right thing and go the right way, even when tempted.

There is such a power in knowing that your father has validated you, by saying, "I love you, you are mine and I am so proud of you." When a person knows this, it helps them carry a sense of wisdom to do right because they know their father is watching and they want to be able to say, "Daddy, I made you proud by making wise decisions like you would."

God wants to heal father wounds so that the children who have been affected by this issue, who are now parents and even grandparents, their children and grandchildren can grow up to help turn America back to God!

SETTLING THE IDENTITY ISSUE

Jesus Christ, the Son of God, came to show us the way to discover who we are.

He is the way, the truth and the life (John 14:6). In Him we can settle the identity issue and enter into the peace of knowing who we are in Christ. Let's look deeper into this truth found in Ephesians 1:5:

God decided in advance to adopt us into his own family by bringing us to himself through Jesus Christ. This is what he wanted to do, and it gave him great pleasure.

Lean in close and hear this everlasting God, who is love, speak this truth to you …

It brought pleasure to God to send Jesus to get you, pick you out and bring you back to Him so that He could adopt you as His own.

I think it's really important that we understand the power of adoption from the biblical perspective and not from a modern-day or perhaps an American one. When scripture tells us that we were adopted as sons, it literally speaks of being placed in the same position as one born into a family with regards to rights, inheritance and legitimacy. In essence, because of what Jesus did and through His work on the cross, you can know that you have been positioned as a SON! You and I are joint heirs to the Father's entire Kingdom as it says in Romans 8:16,17 NKJV: *"The Spirit Himself bears witness with our spirit that we are children of God, **and if children, then heirs** – heirs of God and joint heirs with Christ."*

If you are in Christ, then you are a son of God the Father! Now again, this includes male and female. It's funny because as a woman, you have to get used to being a son; and as a man, you have to get used to being a bride as in the bride of Christ, but there is no gender in Christ Jesus.

Live Like a Son

Why is it so important for you to know your identity? You have to know who you are as a son before you can release your faith to receive what belongs to you.

As I stated earlier, as a believer in Christ, you are born again and have now become a son and a joint heir with Christ. This means you have to stop thinking like a poor, illegitimate son, but like the son of a King. The curse has to be broken off of your mind. There is no lack in your Father's Kingdom, and it is His good pleasure to give it to you (Luke 12:32).

When I know who my heavenly Father is, I understand what belongs to me as a son. We don't have to sit at the back of the bus anymore, because our Daddy owns the bus line. I don't have to fear Him providing for me or protecting me. My children never ever wake up and wonder if there is food in the pantry, or when they sit down to eat, they expect food to hit the table because they know their father has purchased food for them. They are not afraid at night because they know that Daddy is in the house. We have security because we know that nothing can separate us from God's love and nothing can change the fact that we are His. He promised He would never leave us or forsake us (Hebrews 13:5).

He also said that He would not leave us orphaned. He adopted us through the blood of God's firstborn Son. Romans 8:29 NKJV says, *"For whom He foreknew, He also predestined to be conformed to the image of His Son, that He might be the firstborn among many brethren."* Jesus was the firstborn of many brothers, speaking of male and female. He was God's first Son, and now God has many sons and daughters – those of us who are in Christ; those of us who have placed our faith in the work of Jesus on the cross and in His resurrection.

Perhaps you are saying to yourself, "I don't feel like I am where I need to be as a son or daughter. I don't feel like I measure up." Let this scripture remind you of the work He is doing in you.

But to all who believed him and accepted him, he gave the right to become children of God. They are reborn – not with a physical birth resulting from human passion or plan, but a birth that comes from God (John 1:12,13).

If you receive Jesus, He gives you the right to become a child of God. Don't get hung up in your past. Don't get caught up in hitting the replay button in your mind over all your mistakes. Simply hit the delete button and understand that you are becoming. You are not what you are going to be, but you are definitely not what you used to be and definitely are not where you deserve to be. God sees you as a completed work in Christ. He sees your potential and He is working in you right now as you read these words. I am confident the work He began in you, He will complete it until the day of Christ Jesus (Philippians 1:6).

Scriptures give us another instance where Jesus spoke to a crippled man's identity first, then his sin issue and finally his need to be physically healed. Jesus not only saw the man's physical disability. He saw his spiritual disability (sin) as well as his internal disability, his identity. I am sure this man was carrying great shame about his condition.

In Jewish culture, anyone who was crippled could not enter the temple of God to worship. With this came great shame for men especially, who considered it a great honor to be able to enter into the temple of the living God of Israel to worship. Jesus was able to look past his need for physical healing by speaking to his identity issue first. I am sure that he didn't feel like a son of Abraham, even though by birth he was. Notice this encounter in Mark 2:9 NKJV: *"Your sins are forgiven you ... Arise, take up your bed and walk."*

Jesus addressed his identity issue first. He called him "son." In essence, He was saying, "I see that you want to be physically healed, but this issue of identity is much bigger than your physical healing. Son, you are forgiven. Now, get up and take your position as a son."

The enemy has crippled entire generations by attacking men and taking them out of the picture. I truly believe that every person needs to hear those words from Father God in the Son Jesus. "My son, My daughter, you are forgiven. Now rise up from your bed of disability, be healed, get up and take your position as a child of God."

You may have never heard those words before. Maybe you have been abandoned or rejected, never validated, but hear the voice of your Father in heaven as He says, "My son, My daughter, you don't have to be crippled any longer. You are My child, you are forgiven and you are healed. Now pick up your mat, the bed of affliction you have been lying on and go tell your story." The mat represented the man's past (his story) and now God's redemption. Jesus told him to pick it up and carry it so others would see what the Lord had done for him.

In our own lives, Jesus wants to give us validation as children of God, forgive us and heal us. We, in turn, walk in it and now have the confidence as validated children who can tell our story to others, bringing glory to the Father.

I also noticed that Jesus said, "Go to your house." In discussing this with a spiritual father of mine, Dr. Dale Bronner, he said, "If you don't know who you are, you don't know where your house is." As a child of God, we need to know that we have become heirs of the Kingdom of God. We need to know that God has a house. The scriptures teach us that we are God's house and together we are living stones making up one big house. In other words, the house is the Body of Christ. I so love the Body of Christ, the Church of the living God.

I know full well that some people don't like the church or believe in the church, but as for my family and me, we love the church. If it hadn't been for the church or the house of God, I don't know where I would be today. It was the community of authentic Christ followers who gathered where I went back to after straying for over a decade. A house represents power. Even within the American government we see that. We have "The House of Representatives." We have The White House, and we also have God's house! God's power flows from His house, the Church. Power always flows from a house. So go to your house, God's house, the Church. Everything you need is in the Father's house.

Even the prodigal son, while in the pigpen after he came to his senses, knew where to go. He knew where his father's house was and when he went back, his father saw him in the distance and had compassion on him. He embraced him and restored him. He gave him shoes, a ring, a robe and a filet mignon dinner. That's a picture of us and what God the Father wants for us. He does this through His house, the Church.

Yes, there may be some flaky, phony, dead institutions called churches, but always know that there is authentic, Christ-centered, Spirit-led, Spirit-filled churches everywhere in our nation. In fact, now more than ever, they are all over the world. Usually you will find many in every city across our nation with all the church planting that is going on in our world today.

In fact, our church, Turning Point Church, is honored to be a part of a great church planting organization that is planting successful, life-giving churches everywhere in the U.S. You can visit the website to find one near you, the Association of Related Churches, also known as ARC. Please visit www.relatedchurches.com for more information. I strongly encourage you to find your house and go to it. I know from personal experience that God will launch you into your life purpose, your Kingdom purpose, with power from His house, the local church.

Thank God, at least I knew where to go back to after my decade of decadence running from God, much like the prodigal son in Luke 15. But unlike myself, we have a generation of lost sons and daughters who have never been at the Father's house, so they don't know who they are or where to go. This truth is one more reason I believe God has led me to publish this book. It is another way that God is sending this message to all of those in this fatherless generation who may have never been in or a part of a life-giving church before.

Recently, I heard that America is the fourth largest unchurched nation in the world. Only 9 percent of Americans are actively involved in a local church, and that is equal to about 270 million people or so. It is my heart's desire that all who are far from God would hear this invitation to the Father's house. I desire that every person would discover who they are in Christ and that they would know whose they are. I truly believe when you know who you are and whose you are, you will know where the house is.

History Makers

One story that sticks out to me again is from a movie that really touched me. It confirms that a father can help shape the identity of a child regardless of educational, financial, gender or racial barriers. In Director George Tillman Jr.'s movie, "Men of Honor," it is based upon the true-life story about the son of a Kentucky sharecropper, Carl Brashear, who went into the Navy to find a better life. It is clear in this movie how a father's belief and blessing can impact one's life. Fathers can inspire their children to be history makers. Brashear's father gave him a radio as a parting gift with the letters ASNF carved into the side of this old wooden radio. Neither Brashear nor the viewers of the movie knew what these letters meant until the latter part of the film: A Son Never Forgets. "Never quit ... be the best," his father told him and he never forgot. "God put it into my heart, and my father put it in me before I went to the Navy," said Carl Brashear who became the first African-American U.S. Navy Master Chief.

God wants you to be a history maker. God wants you to make a mark on your generation and the generations coming after you. More than that, He wants to validate you today. Pause for a moment, put down this book and simply call out to Him. As you wait, you will hear His words echoing inside the walls of your heart: "You are My son ... You are my daughter in whom I am well pleased." Let those loving words of truth from your Father be deposited deep within your soul, so deep that when the enemy tries to question you on your identity you can simply ignore him just like Jesus did.

You need to memorize and quote the same scriptures we looked at in this chapter, settling forever the issue of who you are and whose you are! This is your identity, so reclaim it by accepting it and declaring it over your life! From this day forward, you now know who you are. You are a son or daughter of Almighty God the Father, and you know that you are His forever, no matter what. Nothing can separate you from Him again. Nothing!

Pass It On

And now as a son or a daughter, if you have children, regardless of their ages, you need to validate them. I know we get busy building our business or ministry, but we have to put on the brakes and look at the generations behind us who are only with us for a short time. Those little ones are only temporary residents in our homes.

Remember, we are not just raising our children. We are raising our grandchildren's parents, and our careers are not more important than that. The devil knows that if a person can understand who they are, whose they are and be validated, it will bring confidence and stability to their life. As children they need to feel that they are legitimate, not unwanted or illegitimate. So go into their bedroom or wherever they may be. If they are grown, then pick up the phone and don't wait another day to tell them who they are and whose they are.

You may not know how because your father never affirmed you. You may be a great big man on the outside, but on the inside there is that little boy needing the affirmation of a father. Perhaps you are a grown woman and maybe even a grandmother, but inside there is still that little girl in you who always wanted to be Daddy's little princess, but you never quite were.

Never forget that you are the son whom He loves, or if you are female, you are His princess forever and always.

CHAPTER 4

Ask "What?" Not "Why?"

ALL OF OUR lives typically start out good from birth. We have innocence about us and then life happens. We encounter some hurts, disappointments and we have bad things happen to us. We have all had problems and failures. The truth is that we will continue to have challenges that we face throughout life. However, many times we begin to focus on the wrong thing and we can't get over what happened. We can't move beyond what they did to us. We struggle for years and years asking ourselves, "Why me? Why did they do me like that?" We sometimes even question, "Why would a loving God let this happen?"

I have learned that when we face challenges in life, and we will, we need to know that our perspective can change from simply exchanging one small word. Instead of asking *"why"* we should ask *"what."*

This is especially true when it comes to the area of fathers. More than half of us in this country struggle internally with this question, and it's hard to understand a message about a loving God when deep inside we are bent towards asking questions like, "Why did You take my dad? Why did You not give me a very good one?" Instead of asking,

"Why did You let that happen, God?" we can change the question to "what" instead of "why." "*What* is the purpose behind this, God? *What* good are You working in this for me, God, and *what* can I learn from this, God?"

Romans 8:28 tells us that for those of us who have turned to Christ, following Him and loving Him, He causes everything – the good and the bad – to work out for the good. Whatever we face or whatever happens, He will use it to work for our good. That means even the bad things that happen to us, the problems we face and even the injustices set out against us, God somehow in His eternal power and grace will work it in our favor. I am not saying that we can't think, *Why did this happen?* but instead of focusing on why, start asking, "What good can come out of this?"

It reminds me of a story I recently heard about an African king and his best friend. His best friend, when he asked about any decisions the king made or when asked his thoughts about anything, he would say, "This is good." The king would ask him what he thought about going hunting, and his friend would say, "This is good." He would ask him about a decision he made for the country and his friend would say, "This is good." He told him he wanted to go hunting one day, and of course, his friend said, "This is good." While hunting and shooting at an animal, the king's gun backfired, blowing off his thumb. When his friend saw it he said, "It is good." The king angrily said, "This is not good," and threw him in prison for saying so.

A year rolls around and the king goes out to hunt as he often did without his friend who was still in jail, and while hunting he was captured by cannibals who had tied him up and were going to have him for dinner when they noticed his thumb was missing. Being very superstitious they decided not to eat him. They considered him unwholesome because he didn't have all his body parts. They released him and he felt very remorseful for having put his best friend in jail for saying the losing of his thumb was a good thing. He headed straight for the jail to release his friend.

Upon releasing his friend, he tells him of the story and how his missing thumb saved his life. You would think his friend would have been angry and was expecting more than an apology for being locked up for an entire year, but he said to him, "This is good!" What? How could this be good? What could be good about this? His friend gladly expressed that if he had not imprisoned him, he would have been with him hunting and he would have been captured and eaten.

It is all about how we choose to look at life's unfair problems. He decided that no matter what happened to him, it was ultimately a good thing.

Perhaps we can do our best to take on the same perspective as the king's friend did. No matter how bad it was, it could still turn out to be for good in the big picture. I have learned that even when I don't know that God is working, God is working. God the Father is a good God, and no matter what has happened, He is well able to turn it around for good. It may not make sense now, but as we place our trust and keep our eyes on Him, we will see the goodness of the Lord in the land of the living.

BETRAYAL

When we talk about injustice and someone's life being a recipe for bitterness and unforgiveness. I think about a guy named Joseph. He had a dream, and he shared it with his brothers as well as with his father, but they didn't believe it. In fact, his father was insulted and his brothers hated him even more for it.

His brothers decided that they would kill him, but instead they decided to sell him as a slave, fake his death, telling their father that he was gone for good. What a raw deal. Right? Talk about dysfunctional families and sibling rivalry.

This is not a book about the life of Joseph, but I think when we talk about how God can work something out for our good and for His purpose, we have to mention the story of Joseph. He was betrayed by his brothers, sold as a slave, then becomes the best slave in the house of his owner. The owner's wife tried to hook up with him and he bolts on the deal. She lies and has him thrown in prison. Now in prison he becomes a trustee and runs the prison as a model prisoner. Although he is innocent, he still keeps going.

Then he does a favor for the Pharaoh's butler and baker with the promise that they would remember him. That did not happen until two years later. But when it was time, Joseph got his chance and interpreted the king's dream. As a result, he was promoted from prison to the palace in twenty-four hours.

Wow! Talk about a turnaround. One minute you are in a dungy, dark prison with prison clothes on, and the next thing you know, old Joe is a millionaire! They clean him up and put royal clothes on him. Then the Pharaoh puts a ring on his finger and says, "You are the man! You are second in command and you only report to me."

Remember, Joseph was wounded by his family. What started out in a pit of betrayal ended up in a promotion to the palace. My belief is that God didn't do that to Joseph, but He used it to humble him so that Joseph would cry out to God, drawing close to Him.

God sees the big picture. He knows the whole movie, because He wrote it. You may feel like you are in the most painful, tragic scene in the movie of your life. I am sure Joseph felt like that too in more than one scene. Take for instance the pit scene or perhaps the slave scene, then there is the prison scene for nearly ten years or so. Think of it like this. What causes the greatest movies to be categorized as great? Wouldn't you agree that the greatest movies are when tragedy or injustice slams into someone's life, then they dare to believe the impossible and make a comeback? The greatest movies are the ones with the greatest comebacks.

Joseph's story is filled with injustice, betrayal and pain, yet his story didn't end like that. His life ended with him fulfilling his purpose and his potential. He was restored to his father and brothers. He was living in abundance. He had a family of his own and literally saved the world from the famine that hit. That was God's end for Joseph, and Joseph decided to ask "what" instead of "why."

God is not going to let your story end in pain if you dare to believe in His ultimate goodness concerning your destiny. God can and will turn it around. When you have a setback, don't take a step back. Get ready for the comeback. That's whom God pulls for ... the underdog. He loves stories of triumph and victory. He has written the story concerning you, and it's to do you good, to give you hope and a future (Jeremiah 29:11).

I have learned that what may seem like a setback can really be a setup, and that God is preparing you for His plans and purpose for you. God is good, and He is able to work things out for our good in every seemingly negative situation we face in life, which includes the negative situation with a father you may be dealing with currently. God has a purpose, my friend, and if you will trust in that, you too will see His amazing grace unfold in the movie of your life. You will come out on top. You are not going under, but you are going over, because you are an overcomer. God is for you, so who in the world can be against you? Dare to believe that the best is yet to come. He can make all things new for you.

What Will You Do?

As the movie goes on, a famine hits the land, causing Joseph's brothers to come to Egypt for help. Egypt was surviving because of the plan God gave Joseph through interpreting the Pharaoh's dream. His brothers had no idea it was Joseph they approached as they had not seen him in over a decade. Because of what Joseph had gone through in that time, it literally shaped him for this moment. When Joseph had the power to crush those who hurt him, when it was in his power to rightfully wipe out those who wronged him, he chose to see the bigger picture. He chose to see the gracious hand of God in the matter and had compassion on them.

As bad as some people have hurt you, perhaps even your father, never forget that what the devil meant for evil, God will use it for good. Your enemy isn't the person who hurt you. The Bible says that there is one adversary, one thief, and he is Satan. Although he influences and oppresses people to do evil things, our battle is not with people. Our battle, according to 2 Corinthians, is with dark powers and evil rulers in heavenly places.

In life, we will face painful situations, perhaps through some social injustice or some relational dysfunction. From our great pain can come great purpose. Great ministry can be birthed from great misery. When you understand like Joseph did, that all the pain you have gone through wasn't as much about you as it was about helping others, you too can get a glimpse from God's view.

Jacob had died and his brothers thought that now Joseph would bring down the hammer, but look at what Joseph said to them in Genesis 50:20: *You intended to harm me, but God intended it all for good. He brought me to this position so I could save the lives of many people.*

Joseph couldn't hold it against them, because God used it to get Joseph where he was at the moment. Basically, Joseph was extremely grateful to be a powerful man of God, blessed and fulfilling his purpose. He could see that if it weren't for those tragic injustices he went through; he would not be where he was.

God wants the best for you. He wants to take you to a position of victory and blessing. God will take you where you need to go, but not necessarily where you want to go. In considering where you are today, God was not mad at you but madly in love with you. Could it be that God is not punishing you, but He is preparing you for what he has ahead for you? I am sure that Joseph had those days where he was tempted to complain and doubt God's purpose for his life, especially when he chose not to sleep with Potiphar's wife, and yet he still ended up in prison.

Maybe you feel like I did. "God, all I did was obey You," and it seems like you still weren't justified in the matter. Or how about the time when Joseph stepped up to be a witness for God and ministered to the baker and the butler by interpreting their dreams. Two more years passed in prison before the butler remembered Joseph. Joseph was constantly faced with the temptation to complain, but he knew he had a choice. He could complain and remain, or he could continue to praise God, trusting God to raise him to a place of purpose in His Kingdom.

As Americans we are more into microwaving and God is into marinating. Joseph had plenty of time to marinate and absorb this truth into his life as God was shaping his character so he could fulfill God's ultimate plan of saving lives. If God had not done this, then Joseph might have thought it was all about him, when in fact, it was not all about him. It was about saving the lives of many.

We must make a decision. Are we going to become bitter or better? The person who hurt you has caused you to become who you are today. Now you may be able to look at your current situation and say, "Yes, that's why I feel wrecked and messed up." I can totally relate to that way of thinking. It is true, but we also need to see that if we are not careful, we will simply play the blame game. We can stay paralyzed in our current condition, thinking that we can't change. We may think, *We could have had a really great life if my dad hadn't damaged me,* or we can say, "I can't determine what happened to me, but I can determine what happens in me." It's not where you're from that matters as much as where you are going. It's not about how you started but how you finish that really counts.

God has called you upward, higher, to live an amazing abundant life. My prayer for you is that you will believe this truth that somehow God is able to take this mess and turn it into a message. My hope is that you would believe that God can and will turn this situation around to benefit you as well as many others who have been negatively affected in the same way.

I am convinced that God is going to use you to save others, that He will not let this thing that has happened to His child go without impacting other sons and daughters who are still out in the world. God will use your tears and compassion to wreak havoc on the enemy, and hell will pay for what it has done to you.

I see this in the lives of many people of faith that I have met in my journey. I think about my friend, Lisa Williams, who launched and oversees Living Water for girls, a ministry that we support that rescues girls and boys from human sex trafficking in Georgia. Lisa has such a heart for reaching out to these precious sons and daughters from being exploited by this horrible prison. They are picking these girls and boys up, embracing them and providing a safe refuge where healing can begin. The reason why Lisa has such a heart for them is because she was one of them. She moved from saying, "Why God?" to "What God?" She has learned, as we should, that God can bring forth great ministry from great misery, so don't curse your crisis. God can turn any situation around. He can turn your mess into a message of hope and restoration.

One of the greatest liberating truths that I have ever realized was that what I went through, all the pain, fears, tears, feelings of abandonment, rejection, addiction and hopelessness, have been used to help bring healing, not only to my own life, but to the thousands of other lives as well. I have had the privilege of encouraging thousands towards faith in Jesus Christ. That's the bigger picture we have to look at when thinking about the injustice and hurt we have experienced from our fathers. God didn't cause them to do it. God didn't plan for them to do it, but what was meant to harm you, God can turn around to help you for good.

If I hadn't been hurt by my father, who was really hurting inside himself from the lack of good fathering he received as did his father before him, I would not be who I am and where I am today. It has caused me to have a compassion for my children, father, mother, for dads and for every person out there who has been negatively affected by the lack of good fathering. If it hadn't been for the heartache and pain I went through, I would not be the person I am today.

I love what Joseph says when his brothers knew he had every right to crush them and literally punish them. He said in Genesis 50:19, *"Don't be afraid of me. Am I God, that I can punish you?"* Joseph was saying, "Am I God that I can do that?" Joseph understood that only God has the right to punish sin. That's His responsibility and Joseph was simply letting God be God in this situation. That is exactly what we need to do if we want to see God turn it around for good.

Paul, inspired by the Spirit of God, wrote this in Romans 12:19: *"Dear friends, never take revenge. Leave that to the righteous anger of God. For the Scriptures say, 'I will take revenge; I will pay them back,' says the LORD."* In essence, God says that revenge is His job, so let Him take care of it. He won't mess it up like we might if we try to handle it in our own power. I will mess it up every time if I try to take revenge. I know it may seem oh so right, but it's oh so wrong according to God's way. I know you want to chase them down, put the hurt on them and perhaps put them in an arm bar until they tap out. But then you are still set on not releasing them to inflict maximum pain on them for what they did. In our hearts we say, "You are going to pay for what you did to me." That's typically our way of handling things like this, but God's ways are higher, better and they never fail. That's what we call trusting in God when we do things His way.

Have you considered that maybe it's time to believe God at His Word? Have you perhaps come to a place where you see that your way doesn't work? This would be a great place for Dr. Phil to say, "How's that working for you?" I know that I came to a place in my life where I finally understood. I could see that my way wasn't working very well at all. However, God's way has worked exactly as He said it would.

PEACEMAKERS

"Blessed are the peacemakers, for they shall be called sons of God" (Matthew 5:9 NKJV).

Happy are those who make peace. Did you notice that? If we want peace, we have to make it. You can't have peace until you make peace. They shall be called sons of God. Others will know that you are God's by your actions to make peace in that relationship, including the person whom you are releasing from punishment. In this case, your father. It may be hard to believe this, but God loves your father and Jesus went to the cross for him too. God used this opportunity in my life of making peace to witness to my father, even to the point of him being restored to God in a relationship with Jesus for himself.

James, the half brother of Jesus, was also inspired to pen this verse in James 3:18: *"And those who are peacemakers will plant seeds of peace and reap a harvest of righteousness."* In other words, if I will take actions towards peace, then I will bring God's righteous standard into the situation, therefore bringing peace into the middle of it. Jesus is the Prince of Peace, so when you bring Him in, you bring peace and then joy flows from that peace. Doesn't that sound like a good plan? Don't you want to have peace and not the inner turmoil that you have been tolerating for so long? It's time to change that and, my friend, what you tolerate you will never change, so make peace today!

HOW DO I MAKE PEACE?

You make peace through reconciliation. Forgiveness is releasing a person from the punishment they deserve for what they did to you. It is giving up your right to punish them. God says He wants us to reconcile with Him and with those who have wronged us. "Reconcile" means to bring the balance to ZERO. If you reconcile your bank statement, then you bring the balance to zero. The only way to make peace is to bring the balance to zero.

That's why conflict resolution rarely works. You don't resolve conflict in a relationship; you have to reconcile conflict. Think about it like this. Jesus didn't *resolve* our sin, He *reconciled* our sin. He came and shed His blood on the cross. In doing that, He brought our huge debt balance to a zero balance. Second Corinthians 5:19 says, *"For God was in Christ, reconciling the world to himself, no longer counting people's sins against them. And he gave us this wonderful message of reconciliation."*

Christ wiped away our balance and brought it to zero, so now God says, "I want you to do the same. Bring their balance to a zero." Some are thinking, *Michael, you are asking the impossible.* You have to trust the principle of God's Word in this matter, because it works! However, you can't reconcile until you have been reconciled. You have to be reconciled to God yourself first, and then that love gives you the capacity to love as with Joseph and even in my case. Until I receive that love, I can't give it away. When you turn your heart to God, a miracle takes place. God will do the supernatural as you receive His love and then go in faith to make peace. You will see that *"God's way is perfect, and all the Lord's promises prove true"* (Psalm 18:30).

As a teenager and a young man in my early twenties, I was angry with my dad. I would gladly want to cause him pain if I could. Hurting people tend to want to hurt others, because as the old saying goes, misery loves company. I was living in pain, subtly holding a grudge, living life with a chip on my shoulders. That chip would eventually become a boulder that was literally too heavy to carry, the reason being, I was never designed to carry such a burden, but Jesus was. He is the One who carried our burdens to the cross.

When I began to understand the nature of our merciful God and as He began to heal my own heart, I was faced with this opportunity with my own father. I could have held on to the anger for what had happened in our past or I could do what God wanted to do. God wanted me to reconcile, by bringing his balance to a zero. I am convinced that as I released my dad from his debt that God continued to heal me as well as my father. I believe that it's when we choose to hang on to hurts that they are empowered to hang on to us, weighing us down from moving forward into what God has for us in the next scene of our lives.

Joseph understood that it was God alone who could punish someone for their sin. The just and merciful God who would send His own Son to die for guilty people who deserved to be judged, He would give the opportunity to be cleared of all charges. We deserve hell and we get heaven. We get grace for our guilt and forgiveness for our failures.

Manasseh

We cannot allow our hurts or circumstance from our past to rob us of the great future God holds for us. We have to forgive and move forward. When Joseph had a son, he named him Manasseh, which means "to forget." The reason is that he said, *"God has made me forget all my troubles and all my father's family"* (Genesis 41:51). God is certainly more powerful than our past, no matter how bad it was. He can make us forget the pain much like a mother forgets the pain of childbirth once the child is born. He makes us forget, not by erasing the memory, but by taking the sting and paralyzing effect out of it.

Joseph went through tremendous pain over a period of thirteen years, but God's grace and love restored him and blessed him to such a degree that when he tried to identify with the pain, it was as if it had never happened. In other words, he was able to focus on God's goodness in such a way that he could forget the injustices he had previously gone through.

I can tell you from my own life that all the pain that hell unleashed on me since I was a child, God has removed it far from me over the last seventeen years. I look back in the wake of this last decade and a half as a truly born-again follower of Jesus Christ. I have been set free from sin, addictions, depression, hopelessness and loneliness. I have been healed of rejection and given purpose. I have been able to encourage thousands of people with my testimony. I have seen God restore my mother as well as my father. I have been blessed with a beautiful, godly wife, three amazing children and now pastor a young, thriving church with a great future. God did it all and He has blessed me so much that I can hardly remember the pain of my father's house.

My friend, God is no respecter of persons, which means that if He did it for Joseph, He will do it for you too! If He could do it for someone like me, then I have no doubt He can do it for you too. God can bring you to such a place of grace and blessing that it separates you from your past as you see the big picture through His eyes. God wants you to give birth, figuratively speaking, to a Manasseh. "Manasseh" represents God's never-ending love for us and that He will bring us to our destiny. He will separate us from all the pain of our earthly father's house from when we were children. God will restore all the years the enemy stole from you and pour it out on you, your children and your children's children to a thousand generations! He will cause you to forget if you will commit to be a peacemaker and leave the outcome of the movie to Him.

God says in Isaiah 43:18,19 NIV, *"Forget the former things; do not dwell on the past. See, I am doing a new thing! Now it springs up; do you not perceive it?"* God is saying to you, "Don't remember the former things; behold, I will do a new thing. It is going to spring up. Don't you sense it?" I believe you can sense what God is saying to you concerning this matter, and I want to confirm it to you. This is God's will for your life, so do what He says and watch what He does.

Paul echoes this truth by saying, "This one thing I do is *forget* what's behind me and I press toward the goal in front of me" (Philippians 3:13,14). I truly believe that in Christ's mercy and God's plans for us that our best days are always in front of us, not behind us. It will just keep getting better and better. So make your move! Forget the past, be reconciled and then reconcile with your dad.

Be a peacemaker and move closer to your purpose in helping to bring healing to the lives of those who haven't heard yet of this marvelous grace we have in Christ!

One of my all-time favorite songs is "Moving Forward" by Ricardo Sanchez. The song fits perfectly for closing this chapter:

> I'm not going back,
> I'm moving ahead.
> I'm here to declare to you,
> my past is over.
> In You,
> all things are made new.
> Surrendered my life to Christ,
> I'm moving ... moving forward.

Isn't it time for you to move forward into what God has for you? Isn't it time to realize that yesterday's gone? Yesterday ended last night. Yesterday's gone. So now take a step forward, one foot in front of the other, move towards God's best for you!

CHAPTER 5

You Can Call Me Daddy

ERNEST HEMINGWAY ONCE wrote a short story called "The Capital of the World." In it, he told the story of a father and his teenage son who were at odds with one another. The son's name was Paco. He had wronged his father. As a result, in his shame, he had run away from home.

In the story, the father searched all over Spain for Paco, but still he could not find the boy. Finally, in the city of Madrid, in a last desperate attempt to find his son, the father placed an ad in the daily newspaper. The ad read: *"PACO, MEET ME AT THE HOTEL MONTANA. NOON TUESDAY. ALL IS FORGIVEN. PAPA."*

The father in Hemingway's story prayed that the boy would see the ad; and then maybe, just maybe, he would come to the Hotel Montana. On Tuesday, at noon, the father arrived at the hotel. When he did, he could not believe his eyes.

An entire squadron of police officers had been called out in an attempt to keep order among eight hundred young boys. It turned out that each one of them was named Paco. And each one of them had come to meet his respective father and find forgiveness in front of the Hotel Montana.

Eight hundred boys named Paco had read the ad in the newspaper and had hoped it was for them. Eight hundred Pacos had come to receive the forgiveness they so desperately desired. This beautiful story illustrates the great truth that Jesus shared in His Parable of the Prodigal Son. Just as there are many, many Pacos in Hemingway's story, so there are innumerable prodigals in the world today.

In truth, all of us are prodigals. All of us have run away from God. *"We all,"* as the Scriptures say, *"like sheep, have gone astray"* (Isaiah 53:6 NIV).

Fortunately, God has not given up on us. He has made the first move and taken the initiative in reaching His arms out to us. He searches for us. He never gives up on us. He longs day and night for us to come home. And if and when we do, He is overjoyed. He embraces us. He forgives us. He restores us all because He loves us.

When I read that story, it really hit me in my gut. First off, it reminded me that when a father's heart turns toward his child, that child's heart turns to him. This truth is confirmed in Malachi 4:6 NIV: *"He will turn the hearts of the fathers to their children...."* The father's heart turns first. Think about how God is the One who has turned His heart toward us through His Son Jesus Christ.

As we read the Scriptures, I find it interesting that in the Old Testament God was known as Yahweh, El Shaddai, Jehovah and many other names that describe His character and nature. Yet when we read the New Testament, He is simply referred to as "Father." I love the fact that God sent His Son to reveal Himself as Father. It is as if all the Old Testament names were all rolled up into one that describes what a true father should be.

As God revealed Himself as Father in the New Testament, it really goes even deeper in the sense of the intimacy that He wants to have with us. When Jesus was praying in the garden, we see a new intimate expression that Jesus uses when engaging with the Father as recorded in Mark 14:36 NKJV: *"Abba, Father, all things are possible for You. Take this cup away from Me; Nevertheless, not what I will, but what You will."* "Abba" was an intimate word that Hebrews used much like the word we use today, "Daddy."

If I introduce my dad, I would say, "This is my father," but when I speak to him or call him, I would call him Dad. I believe that is the intimate expression Jesus used because He was showing us how close our Father wanted to be to us. He wanted us to understand that He is not just our God or some impersonal deity, but actually as He is, our Daddy!

I can remember the first time I heard my oldest son, Michael Jr., call me Daddy. It really causes your chest to swell and your eyes to fill with tears. I love for my kids to call me Daddy, and I think God likes it when we call Him Daddy!

Genesis 1:26 tells us that we were made in the image of God. It literally means that we came from within His very nature. In this same chapter, He created water and then commanded fish to come from within the water. He then commanded that the trees come from the dirt. You have to understand that we came forth from the very image of Daddy God. He is our Source. Just like a fish can't live out of water and a tree can't live out of the soil, neither can we live out of the intimate fellowship and presence of our Daddy.

As never before in the history of America, we need daddies to be healed and revealed. Likewise, there has never been a greater need for the understanding of God as Daddy than now. We have seen an entire generation grow up without the active presence of a father.

In 1960 only 9 percent of children lived without a father in their home, but today over 50 percent of children will live without Daddy in the house. Seventy-three percent of Americans said fatherlessness is the greatest social family problem. Twenty-five million children today are physically fatherless; millions more have a father present, but they are emotionally fatherless.

As I look around our country today, I see men who had no father growing up that are now fathers themselves. For instance, look at President Obama, who has grown up without truly knowing his father. He now has two children and he is the most powerful man in the world. As Senator Barack Obama, he was asked this question from a man seated in the crowd at the Washington County fairgrounds: "What would you say is the most painful and character-building experience of your life that puts you in a position to make important decisions of life and death and the well-being of our country?"

"I would say the fact that I grew up without a father in the home." What that meant was, "I had to learn very early on to figure out what was important and what wasn't, and exercise my own judgment and in some ways to raise myself."

I truly believe that many men want to be good fathers, but they may not know how or believe that they can be. Perhaps you are a father or will be one day, I want to encourage you, because if God can heal my life and my father wounds, he can heal yours too. If He has empowered me to become a good father, He can do it for you too. Please understand, there are no perfect fathers, but we can be humble enough to turn to Father God to allow Him to do that work in us. Today I am still learning every day to be my very best. You can start today and know that yesterday ended last night. If you have blown it for years, it's never too late to start on that road to reconciliation. God can heal your life. He can cause rapid recovery and radical restoration in your life and in the lives of your children!

Maybe you didn't have a great dad. According to stats, the majority of us did not, but you know what? You can become the dad you never had! That's exactly what I, as well as millions of other guys who grew up without an active father in their life, have decided to do.

Maybe you have kids now and you feel like a failure. You are reading this book right now because something stirred in you when you read the title. That's proof that you care and that God can still do a miracle in spite of your mistakes! You are not a failure until you quit trying. I know that God can turn your mistake into a miracle, because He did it for me, and He is no respecter of persons. So if you will believe, He can do it for you too.

Orphans, Slaves and Sons

In Luke 15 we see a story of a son who wanted his inheritance before his dad died. He was basically saying that he wished his dad was dead so he could get his money. He wanted to do things on his own. He thought he knew best for his life and he was set on proving it, if his father would only give him his stuff that he rightfully deserved.

This loving dad gave his ungrateful son his cut of his inheritance before the legal time of his death. This son heads out to prove that he knows best for his life like most of us do when we are younger, only to prove that too much too soon only destroys us. He spent all he had on wild friends and wild living. This young Jewish boy finds out that going against his father's wisdom and way of life led him to poverty in a pigpen. Jewish boys had no business being anywhere near a pig as it was unlawful to eat pigs, much less consider working with them and eating their food.

The Bible says this young man came to his senses and remembered the warmth and provision of his father's house. He realized he had blown it and wanted to make things right with his dad. In fact, he realized he had sinned against his God and his dad. At least in his darkest moment, he knew that everything started to go south when he went against his father and left his father's house. He knew he needed to get back to Dad's place. In his mind, he decided that he wasn't worthy to be called a son and that perhaps he could be like a slave if his father would extend him some mercy.

I love the picture of this loving father who was watching daily to see if his wayward son would come home. As the young man was returning, his father saw him in the distance and ran to meet him, embraced him (even though he probably reeked of the pigpen) and kissed him. The son begins to explain and apologize, but this father's love is so deep that he never even acknowledges it. Instead, he calls for a robe, a ring and shoes for his boy. If that wasn't enough, he summoned his staff to kill a fattened calf. They were about to have a party with a filet mignon barbecue!

I noticed that the heart of the son changed. He was selfish and prideful before leaving, saying, "Give me." He returned broken from the world and life in the pigpen, saying, "Make me like one of your servants."

Spiritual orphans live with the mentality of, "Give me what is mine," feeling owed something. Spiritual orphans don't trust father's leadership. In fact, they don't trust spiritual authority or church leadership for that matter. Spiritual orphans don't commit to the house because they feel they know better and there is no need for spiritual covering. Spiritual orphans struggle with commitment, not just to one church (house), but really in every area of their lives.

Physiologists now say that many twenty something year olds have no hope in anything today. They can't keep jobs or stay in long-term relationships because of trust issues. They have been coined "the lost decade." I believe it's because they have never had anyone give them a reason to believe or trust in the Father's house. In fact, many don't know anything about Father's house because they don't know who they are. They don't trust in pastors because many of them have never had any interaction with godly men of integrity, especially that of a father. They have never felt Father's love or known hope in Him. They have only had themselves to trust in, and they have never had anyone speak to their potential, so they really haven't had a reason to trust anyone.

Orphans bounce from job to job, relationship to relationship and church to church. This young man in the story was not an orphan, but he thought like one. He wanted his inheritance now and was really saying, "I wish you were dead so I could have my money and live like an orphan with deep pockets." But eventually his money ran out and so did his so-called friends.

Even though the son who returned home wanted to be a slave, his dad wouldn't let him because he was not a slave but a son. His desire was right when he said, "I don't deserve to be a son," and it's true. He didn't deserve it and neither do we.

What about the older son? He was performance based because he said, "I have always done right and I never got a party." He thought works or performance maintained his position. He said, "Look at me, Dad, how good I am doing." Slaves are those who are sons of the father who think they maintain their position through performance. In other words, always doing good works to try to get father's approval and attention. They think, "If I do this or that, God will love me more. If I am good, then I will get his favor. If I serve more, if I tithe and go to church more, then he will keep me around as a son."

I used to be like this. Please understand, I am all for a changed heart touched by grace producing good works. Works and faith together are the proof of living faith, according to James. When I came to the Lord as a young Christian, I worked harder than anybody as a volunteer and even as a staff pastor. In my mind I was working and doing good because I thought that it would please God and He would allow me to hang around Him. Even though I was a son and everything in the house belonged to me via my Father, I was like this older son who was still thinking that his works gave him position or that he earned his place as a son.

I have three children, Michael Jr., Presley and Madelyn. When my wife gave birth to Michael, Presley followed after twenty-six months, then Madelyn followed a short thirteen months after that. We had three children that were ages three, one and newborn. Presley was born one month before we planted our first church and Madelyn came a year later. We were in an intense season of our lives. We were new parents and new senior pastors all at once it seemed. The pressure was very intense at times with these wonderful blessings that God entrusted us with all at once. Being a new father was one of the greatest joys of my life. Words can't express the deep love I have for these children that God has given to my wife and me. My children are high octane and strong willed to put it mildly. I am certain that they get it all from their mother. Not really, it's mostly from me that they inherited these God-given traits. As you can imagine, that intensified our household in various moments.

Over a decade later, as my children have grown, one of many things that I have constantly sown into their hearts is that they are mine and they are Turners for life. They don't wake up every day wondering if they still belong to me. They know that they are my sons and she is my daughter no matter what. Even on their worst days, they still belong to me and their positions as sons and daughter are forever secured. Their positions aren't based on performance, so they can rest in the security of peace knowing that nothing can ever change that.

This truth has revolutionized my life and freed me from the slavery of worrying about messing it all up again and having to earn my place in the house. I know who I am. I am a son and nothing can ever, ever change that. Even though I have been entrusted with a wife, a family and a church, it's not who I am. I am a husband, a father and a pastor. That is what I do, but it's not who I am. I am a son first and foremost. It's out of that place that all else flows to me and through me from my Daddy to empower me to be. In this manner, I am empowered to effectively fulfill those roles in my life.

In order to be a great father I have to know how to be a great son. Knowing that I am a son fulfills me, because I know who I am and whose I am. My children will grow to be great parents, partly because they experienced being fathered and they learned to be great sons and a daughter first, which is God's will from the beginning. That is God's will for you too. He wants to be your Daddy. It pleased Him to adopt us as Ephesians 1:5 tells us, *"God decided in advance to adopt us into His own family by bringing us to Himself through Jesus Christ. This is what He wanted to do, and it gave Him great pleasure."*

God initiated the contact to reach out to us and bring us to Himself, and it brings Him pleasure. Have you ever known that or dwelt on the fact that you bring pleasure to your Daddy? You have to understand that as a son, everything the Father has belongs to you. You can't earn it or be good enough to keep it, you simply receive it and enjoy it. I am blown away by the picture of this father that Jesus paints for us. This father didn't browbeat or tell him, "I told you so." He ran to him, embraced him and kissed him. Then he put shoes on him because only sons, not slaves, wore shoes. He places a robe on him just as the father covers us and wraps His robe of righteousness around us to cover the stench of our sin we had from the pigpen. Then he places the ring on his finger to seal the fact that he was a son by restoring his authority as an heir.

Friend, when you come home to the father's house, you are not an orphan nor a slave, but a son and not just a son but an heir and a joint heir with Christ as recorded in Galatians 4:4-7:

But when the right time came, God sent his Son, born of a woman, subject to the law. God sent him to buy freedom for us who were slaves to the law, so that he could adopt us as his very own children. And because we are his children, God has sent the Spirit of his Son into our hearts, prompting us to call out, "Abba, Father." Now you are no longer a slave but God's own child. And since you are his child, God has made you his heir.

The law of God (the Ten Commandments) shows us that we need the grace of a Savior. We will never be good enough. Even while I was at my worst, living for myself, I still had a Father who loved me and prepared an inheritance for me.

God sent His Son Jesus to die for you so that you wouldn't have to be a slave any longer but a son. He even sent His Spirit into your heart so that you would know Him as Abba or Daddy. When you come back to the Father's house, even though you may not feel worthy, come anyway. The bad news is that you are not worthy. The good news is that Jesus paid the price so you could be worthy. When you turn to Jesus Christ for forgiveness, that is the Father running to you to embrace you, kiss you and cover your selfish stench with His righteousness. That's amazing grace. You are no longer an orphan. You are no longer a slave. You are a son and nothing can ever change that.

My children never wonder or worry if I am ever going to remove my name from their birth certificate. If you have placed your trust in Christ, then nothing can change the fact that you are a son! Say that out loud: "I am a son." Never forget it. It's who you are. God says, "Welcome home. All that I have is yours." It is His good pleasure to give you the Kingdom. God says, "You can call me Daddy."

In Philip Yancey's book, *What's So Amazing About Grace?* there is a story that truly illustrates what kind of Daddy God is really like. A young girl grows up on a cherry orchard just above Traverse City, Michigan. Her parents, a bit old-fashioned, tend to overreact to her nose ring, the music she listens to and the length of her skirts. They ground her a few times, and she seethes inside. "I hate you!" she screams at her father when he knocks on the door of her room after an argument.

That night she acts on a plan she has mentally rehearsed scores of times. She runs away. She has visited Detroit only once, on a bus trip with her church youth group, to watch the Tigers play. Because newspapers in Traverse City report in lurid detail about the gangs, the drugs and the violence in downtown Detroit, she concludes that Detroit is probably the last place her parents will look for her. California, maybe, or Florida, but not Detroit.

Her second day there she meets a man who drives the biggest car she has ever seen. He offers her a ride, buys her lunch and arranges a place for her to stay. He gives her some pills that make her better than she has ever felt before. She was right all along, she decides. Her parents were keeping her from all the fun.

The good life continues for a month, two months, a year. The man with the big car – she calls him "Boss" – teaches her a few things that men like. Since she is underage, men pay premium for her. She lives in a penthouse, and orders room service whenever she wants. Occasionally she thinks about the folks back home, but their lives seem so boring and provincial that she can hardly believe she grew up there.

She has a brief scare when she sees her picture printed on the back of a milk carton with the headline, "Have you seen this child?" But by now she has blonde hair, and with all the makeup and body-piercing jewelry she wears, no one would mistake her for a child. Besides, most of her friends are runaways, and nobody squeals in Detroit.

After a year, the first signs of illness appear, It amazes her how fast the boss turns mean. "These days we can't mess around," he growls, and before she knows it, she is out on the street without a penny to her name. She still turns a couple of tricks a night, but they don't pay much, and all the money goes to support her habit.

When winter blows in, she finds herself sleeping on metal grates outside the big department stores. "Sleeping" is the wrong word – a teenage girl at night in downtown Detroit can never relax her guard. Dark bands circle her eyes. Her cough worsens, and one night as she lies awake listening for footsteps, all of a sudden everything about her life looks different. She no longer feels like a woman of the world. She feels like a little girl, lost in a cold and frightening city. She begins to whimper. Her pockets are empty and she's hungry. She needs a fix. She pulls her legs tight underneath her and shivers under the newspapers she has piled atop her cloak.

Something jolts a synapse of memory and a single memory and a single image fill her mind of May in Traverse City when a million cherry trees bloom at once, with her golden retriever dashing through the rows and rows of blossomy trees in chase of a tennis ball. "God, why did I leave?" she says to herself, and pain stabs at her heart. "My dog back home eats better than I do now." She's sobbing and she knows in a flash that more than anything else in the world she wants to go home.

Three straight phone calls, three straight connections with the answering machine. She hangs up without leaving a message the first two times, but the third time she says, "Dad, Mom, it's me. I was wondering about maybe coming home. I'm catching a bus up your way, and it will get there about midnight tomorrow. If you are not there, well, I guess I'll just stay on the bus until it hits Canada."

It takes about seven hours for a bus to make all the stops between Detroit and Traverse City, and during that time, she realizes the flaws in her plan. What if her parents are out of town and missed the message? Shouldn't she have waited another day or so until she could talk to them? And even if they are home, they probably wrote her off as dead long ago. She should have given them some time to overcome the shock.

Her thoughts bounce back and forth between those worries and the speech she is preparing for her father. "Dad, I'm sorry. I know I was wrong. It's not your fault; it's all mine. Dad, can you forgive me?" She says the words over and over, her throat tightening even as she rehearses them. She hasn't apologized to anyone in years. The bus has been driving with lights on since Bay City. Tiny snowflakes hit the pavement rubbed worn by thousands of tires and the asphalt steams. She has forgotten how dark it gets at night out here. A deer darts across the road and the bus swerves. Every so often, a billboard sign posts the mileage to Traverse City. Oh, God.

When the bus finally rolls into the station, its air brakes hissing in protest, the driver announces in a crackly voice over the microphone, "Fifteen minutes, folks. That's all we have here." Fifteen minutes to decide her life. She checks herself in a compact mirror, smooths her hair and licks the lipstick off her teeth. She looks at the tobacco stains on her fingertips, and wonders if her parents will notice if they're there.

She walks into the terminal not knowing what to expect. Not one of the thousand scenes that have played out in her mind prepare her for what she sees. There, in the concrete wall and plastic chairs bus terminal in Traverse City, Michigan, stands a group of forty brothers and sisters and great aunts and uncles and cousins and a grandmother to boot. They are all wearing goofy party hats and blowing noisemakers, and taped across the entire wall of the terminal is a computer-generated banner which reads, "Welcome home!"

Out of the crowd of well-wishers breaks her dad. She stares out through the tears quivering in her eyes like hot mercury and begins the memorized speech. "Dad, I'm sorry. I know…." He interrupts her. "Hush, child. We've got no time for that. No time for apologies. You'll be late for the party. A banquet is waiting for you at home." This is exactly the way God feels for us. More specifically, the way He feels about you. You see, when Jesus told the story of the prodigal son, it wasn't about some fictitious father and a son. It was a story about God and a story about you, a story about me.

If you have not trusted Christ as your Lord and Savior, my sincere hope is that you will come home to the Father. I hope that you would know the peace and joy that come with having been forgiven by God. If you have not, my friend, the Father's invitation to come home still stands. Even now, He is waiting for you. He longs for your return and is waiting to let you off the hook. He will not beat you down; rather, He will embrace you, restore you and bless you. He wants you to know that no matter what you have done or where you have been, He still loves you. He wants you to know that you can call Him Daddy!

CHAPTER 6

You Want Me to Do What?

IN THE PROCESS of healing and restoration for our lives, we must understand the life-giving power of forgiveness and the destructive force of unforgiveness which can be stealth like in nature, robbing us of our joy and strength. Unforgiveness leads to bitterness, it traps us and even tortures us. Sometimes we have been wounded so deeply by our father's actions or the lack thereof that we want to make him pay for what he did. We may try to lash out or ignore a father's attempt to reconcile after we are grown up, or older I should say, because it seems to feel right and it feels good. We want to punish him for hurting us.

The truth is, we can never overcome hurt by hurting. The Bible is clear when it says we don't overcome evil with evil, but we overcome evil with good. Good always triumphs in the end. I know it may sound corny to say that good guys always win, but it's true. Doing what is right, even when it's hard or seemingly illogical, always wins out. Jesus told us to love not only those who love us, but to love our enemies and to bless those who curse us.

When I follow this advice, it's amazing how therapeutic it is for me in my heart. I have found this to be true when dealing with our fathers. I know firsthand how deep the wounds of a father can be. Some believe that time heals all wounds, but that is simply not true. For many of us the wounds we received from our fathers are as fresh today as they were thirty years ago. Even after reconciling with my father and growing in my relationship with Jesus Christ, those scars are still tender as any scar tissue can be.

In my own life, I remember when I was born again and began to follow Jesus Christ. It was then that I discovered the hidden truth of a lot of my dysfunction was from the absence of my father in my life. At first I experienced anger, resentment and unforgiveness. The closer I walked with God, the more I was healed and the more I understood about the root of the generational dysfunction that had been passed down from previous generations. I heard this teaching on forgiveness and decided to extend it to my own dad.

In 1997 my father was going through a bout doctors diagnosed as depression, and I felt the Lord leading me to reach out to him. It started by me picking up the phone and calling him first. If there was going to be restoration and forgiveness, I realized I had to be the one to initiate the process. I started to understand that my dad must have felt as if he was failing in life and may have wanted to call me. He just didn't have the courage to do so. I would try to encourage him with the Word of God without seeming like I was preaching to him. So over the course of a few weeks, I decided to stop by for a visit, and I also gave him some teaching tapes to listen to. I knew the power of the spoken Word had changed my life, and God helped me to sincerely desire to help my father.

I noticed that as I took the focus off of my pain and started feeling his, it changed my heart. I noticed a difference in the way our conversations went and he was laughing again.

As the weeks went by, I remembered growing up as a child that his favorite cake was coconut, so I bought one along with a personalized Bible. Over the course of the next few months, my dad was reading the Bible every day and watching different speakers on Christian television. We began to share truths from God's Word, and amazingly we had a relationship again.

It wasn't too long before he came to visit the church I started working for as my first ministry position. One day my father told me that he wanted to get baptized and he wanted me to do it. I was so humbled and grateful to God for honoring me with the opportunity to be able to baptize my dad. God was writing an amazing story of restoration in my life. I could have never dreamed up something so powerful as that.

In early 1998 I was to be married, and at my rehearsal dinner, the healing continued as my father stood up in a room of thirty people or so and publicly thanked me for leading him back to Christ.

"The glory of children is their fathers" (Proverbs 17:6 ESV). I was so proud of my dad that day for having the guts to stand up in a room of people he didn't even know and honor me like he did. I want to take a quick pause to say this: Dad, I will never forget that, and I know that you did that for me. That was the greatest gift you have ever given me. Thank you." I didn't say it, but I knew who the credit belonged to. It wasn't me but my Father in heaven who was the real hero in the story.

I want you to think about this for a moment. How was God able to work like He did in this story? I can tell that it all happened because I went against my wounds and anger. I knew that hadn't worked and that

God in His infinite wisdom was showing me a better way. His way – love. Love never fails. So as I decided to follow the voice of God's love, forgiveness flowed from my heart. I chose to extend the mercy and grace that I had received from Jesus Christ.

Love is not a feeling. It's an action. Love is giving someone what they need, not what they deserve. I deserved hell and I got heaven. I deserved to be judged and I got mercy instead. Love is not doing something because you feel it. It's an act of your will to do the right thing. In fact, it's not about what you feel. Rather, it's doing something for someone else so they feel love. When we don't feel like doing something and we do it anyway, it's actually a greater expression of love.

Did you know that when Jesus died for you, there was a moment when He didn't want to do it? In fact, there were three separate accounts in scripture where He prayed to the Father and asked if there was any other way to redeem us other than Him laying down His sinless life for sinful mankind. He didn't want to endure the whipping, the beating, the crown of thorns, the road of suffering and the cross. Even while on the cross He asked the Father to forgive those who did this to Him because they knew not what they did.

I really believe that my father had no idea the weight of what his decisions as a young twenty something would do to his son. I didn't think I could do it, but I could only through Christ, and my friend, I want you to know that you can too. You have a choice and no matter how ugly the story may have been, God can flip the script for the good of both you and your father if you let Him. All you have to do is receive the love and forgiveness of Christ and then give it to your father. It doesn't matter if you don't know where he is or where he lives or if he is alive. I know that with God all things are possible if you will only believe.

You can call out to Him right now wherever you may be and He will answer. If you know where your father is, then pursue him in love and watch God go to work on your behalf.

It is amazing how forgiving we can be as children. Many times, even if our fathers were wrong, we were so forgiving. I know in my own life, it was hard for my mother to understand how I could forgive my dad for the way he treated us. Maybe it was the fact that I hadn't learned that behavior yet. What happens to us as we grow older? Somewhere along the way in our victim mentality culture, we think we have a right to hold a grudge. We think that people owe us and that only leads to wrong thinking. In reality, that simply leaks out into every relationship that we have which leads us to more heartache. I know deep down inside of us, it is that childlike ability to forgive. I encourage you to forgive your father.

Today I am meeting with a great young lady, Valerie, who is a member of our church. She is coming to see me and wants advice on how to approach her father who is in prison. She is willing to take a risk by reaching out to him, a convicted murderer. She is hesitant, but feels the need to reach out to him. She did reach out to him and forgave him. She extended the same love and forgiveness Christ has given to her. I was so very proud of her for having the courage to take the first step towards her dad, even if it meant going into a prison to do it. You go, girl!

On another occasion, I spoke with a young man who had to deal with what has to be one of the greatest offenses any person could possibly go through. He had to decide if he was going to forgive his father. He grew up with a relationship with his dad. He never thought he would have to forgive his father for something that simply seems unforgivable. His father had admitted to molesting this young man's children. His father was in prison when we had this talk, so you can understand this young man's challenge to forgive his father.

As we talked and wept, I encouraged him with what I have found to be true in my life as well. We must forgive our fathers for whatever they have done to us, because it ultimately sets us free as well. The mercy that this young man offered to his imprisoned father blew me away and helped me to put my own situation into perspective. There was repentance and reconciliation in that relationship largely because this son was willing to release his father from the debt he owed.

So for us who have been hurt by our fathers, what can we do? We can make a choice to forgive and to honor our fathers. "You want me to do what??" I know you may be saying, "Wait a second. I can't forgive him and honor him. He deserves to hurt. He deserves pain in return. What goes around comes around. He doesn't deserve to be forgiven. You are right. He doesn't deserve it. This is the core of God's grace and mercy through His Son Jesus Christ. We don't get what we deserve.

All of us have fallen short. We have all made mistakes and transgressed the law of God. Our sins put Jesus Christ on the cross of Calvary. We deserved to be judged by the only Person who was ever totally sinless and righteous. When we should have been judged we found grace and forgiveness. God took our failures and gave us forgiveness. God took our guilt and gave us grace. That is what grace is — undeserved. I am so glad that I didn't get what I deserved. So if we have freely received, then shouldn't we freely give?

We are tempted to make our fathers pay for what they did, and if we are honest, it seems to feel good or make it better, but it doesn't. We want to give them what they deserve. I am so glad that God didn't give me what I deserved. I should have been judged and God could have wiped me off the face of the earth. He had the power to crush me, yet He had compassion on me. He didn't make me pay back what I owed.

When it comes to forgiveness, it is a choice, but it is also a command. When you or I need to forgive, I believe the way we do that is to look beyond the person who hurt us and look to Jesus on a blood-stained cross. I believe that is what God the Father does when He forgives us. I believe He looks past us to the blood of Jesus Christ that was shed, and says, "I forgive you. Your debt is paid, and you owe Me nothing."

You and I have to release our fathers from their debt and free them. When we do not forgive, it leads to bitterness. Bitterness will corrupt your heart, steal your joy and destroy your life as well as the lives of those around you.

To illustrate this truth even further, I read about an eighth grade teacher who wanted to teach her students the effects of being offended. She asked the students to bring in a five-pound bag of potatoes to the school for an experiment. The students were instructed to empty their bags on their desks. The teacher then gave each student one rotten potato to place at the bottom of his or her bag. The bags were refilled with the good potatoes, labeled with each student's name and placed high on a shelf.

In a few days when the bags were checked, the students discovered that some of the potatoes close to the rotten potato at the bottom of the bag were showing signs of decay. Days later, more potatoes were affected. Before long, the entire bag had decayed. All of the potatoes had been "infected" by the one rotten potato.

The point of the experiment was to show the students how keeping company with "a rotten potato" (someone who has allowed himself to become infected with bitterness and negativity over an offense) would affect them. Over time, one person's "rotten" attitude toward life would influence their way of thinking, believing and acting.

When we don't forgive, we are allowing our fathers to still have control over us, so we must free them and that in turn frees us. Forgiveness ultimately benefits us the most, not those we choose to forgive. Forgiveness is not saying what you did to me is all right, but simply says you don't have to suffer for it. Forgiveness is not forgetting, but simply saying, "I give up my right to hurt you for hurting me. You don't owe me anything." How do you do that? You have to realize the bigger picture. It is not our father's fault. It is the fault of the father of lies. It is the fault of the deceiver of old, Satan. The Bible is clear that our battle is not with flesh and blood, but with rulers of darkness. Satan is the thief, not your father. The truth is that if you will look up to your father's father and his father, you will probably get a glimpse of where the trouble began.

I spent the afternoon speaking with another young lady, a member of our church, who was hurting from never dealing with her father. With tears in her eyes, she shared with me about all the times he had rejected her and even chosen her half brother over her many times. She recalled those painful memories of her childhood when her father would promise to pick her up and her bags would be packed, but Dad never came. Now a woman in her early thirties and her father being somewhat older in his years, he recently suffered a massive stroke and is in critical condition. Being a willing daughter, she decided to visit him in his hour of need.

She now has a choice and a chance to forgive him. With tears in her eyes, she explained that to be able to communicate with her, he could blink his eyes. "Do you recognize me?" was her question to him when she came into his hospital room. He would blink to say, "I do. I recognize you, my daughter." I can only imagine what the eyes of this disabled father who couldn't use his words to express his regrets but could only use his eyes to say "I hear you" must have been like. What did he want to say, I wondered.

If like most men who blew it as young fathers, they would say, "I am sorry. I love you. Please forgive me for what I have done to you. Forgive me for not being there for you. I have regretted every painful decision I have made about you."

"What should I do?" was her earnest request. My response was, "Forgive him. You should bless him. You should look through the eyes of our merciful God. I want you to look at his past. I want you to consider the lack of good fathering he may have experienced, because one thing I have learned over the last seventeen years is that everyone, whether they are good or bad, is that way for a reason. We are all simply a product of our environment. Could it be that your dad was blinded by his own sin or his inability to have ever received God's love, much less give it to you?

I know that we can never truly love with that kind of unconditional, never-ending love that comes only from God until we receive that love from Him. We can't give away what we do not have. But here is your chance to be Jesus to your dad, and this could possibly be the defining moment, the key to his eternal destination.

I concluded with, "You will be honoring God. You are never more like God when you forgive someone and overlook an offense."

OFFENDED

In the book, *The Bait of Satan,* which I highly recommend for every Christ follower, author John Bevere teaches a powerful truth concerning offenses. You have to remember that we have one enemy, Satan. He, not our fathers, is the enemy or our souls. He wants to corrupt our hearts like a VIRUS in a computer. He wants our hearts to be bitter and offended. When we harbor unforgiveness, it corrupts our hearts, Proverbs 4:23 says, *"Guard your heart above all else, for it determines the course of your life."* Guard in the sense of protecting your heart from things that try to get in it that cause spiritual heart disease or hardening of the heart.

Jesus constantly spoke about this hardness of heart that wasn't a heart that He desired or one that gives us the quality of life that we desire. He rebuked the religious leaders whose hearts were hardened, causing them to divorce their wives without a cause (Matthew 19:6-8). Then, in Mark 16:14, His own followers didn't believe the report from other disciples that He was alive again, and the hearts of others were hardened against Jesus healing a man with a disability in Mark 3:5.

It is clear from the Scripture that things can harden us and affect our capacity to love and to be loved. When it comes to this issue of unforgiveness, if we don't forgive, then bitterness can grow in our hearts and into not only our lives but in the lives of all those around us as Hebrews 12:15 explains: *"Watch out that no poisonous root of bitterness grows up to trouble you, corrupting many."* God asks us to forgive others, even our fathers, to protect us from the poison of bitterness. God doesn't want us to choose to be bitter, but He wants us to choose to be better. When you forgive, you are better off for it in the end.

Bitterness is a trap of the enemy that comes when we are offended by someone else and we choose to embrace it instead of releasing it from our heart.

It's a Trap

Luke 17:1 NKJV says, *"Then He said to the disciples, 'It is impossible that no offenses should come, but woe to him through whom they do come!'"* The question is not, "Will you encounter offense?" Rather, it is, "How will you respond?"

The word "offense" in the Greek is *skandalon* – a trap that hunters would use with bait to trap animals. They would wait for the animals to go for the bait, and then pull the string to drop the trap. Your enemy, Satan, does the same thing and he uses offenses as the bait. A hunter using a *skandalon* had to be very crafty. If the bird or animal recognized the trap, it would not work. Satan does the same thing with the offenses your father has executed. You and I are most vulnerable to offense by those who are within close proximity of us.

Offenses keep us locked up as if we were surrounded by a fence of iron. The wisest guy who ever lived, next to Jesus, said this about offenses: *"A brother offended is harder to win than a strong city, and contentions are like the bars of a castle"* (Proverbs 18:19 NKJV).

If we want to experience healing and freedom from the hurts of our fathers, we have to be totally forgiven and we have to totally forgive those who hurt us. So let me give you three steps to getting free through forgiveness.

1. Put down the fence.

The offense has become your defense to further hurt, but it has surrounded your heart, hindering your capacity to receive the God-kind of love, much less give it away to others. If we don't deal with offense, it will lead us to hate and that ultimately hurts us since we can't walk in God's love and freedom while entertaining offense. "Hate" means to be void of love – loveless. Again, we can't walk in love and unforgiveness at the same time.

As amazing as the story of restoration between my father and me has been, I also found out that even though some healing took place, I was still very tender in this area of my life. About ten years ago, my father relocated out of state to a small town in Florida. He had only visited me and my family two times in that previous decade. In fact, he had only seen my daughter once as an infant.

We were traveling through the town on our way to Orlando for a family vacation. We decided to reach out to my father. We called to see if he would be interested in meeting us near the highway for dinner on our way back from our trip. He agreed and upon our return trip, we hit some traffic putting us about two hours behind schedule.

My children were really looking forward to seeing him and so was I. At the last minute when we called to let him know what our arrival time would be, he thought it was too late and cancelled. My children didn't take it too well and neither did I. I decided that I wasn't going to subject myself or my children to any more disappointment at the hands of my father. I decided that I would not initiate any more contact with him. If he wanted to reach me, he knew my number.

What I didn't realize is that my hurt had led to an offense. I was offended and defending my heart. Over the months, I didn't hear from him and in the courtroom of my mind I stood my ground justly so. Somehow as I would share that story, I recognized that it was turning into anger. I was holding on to this offense and believing that I had a right to defend my cause so as not to be hurt any more and so my children would not experience that pain again.

Thankfully the Holy Spirit showed me that I was offended, and it was going to cause bitterness to spring up if I didn't deal with it. What is really interesting is that I was at a pastors' conference to learn how to get better as a pastor when God revealed to me that I was on the border of bitterness. I finally agreed with God and I realized that the time to act was when God's loving conviction comes.

After the workshop, I went outside to call my dad. It had been six months or so since we had last communicated. I called him and got right to the point of my call. I explained everything, and to my surprise he said, "I am sorry." Instantly, the offense was gone. I felt it leave me along with a few tears. As I stated earlier, I don't think that tender scar ever totally heals, and honestly, I am glad because I think it keeps me tender and broken towards all those who have experienced the same pain as I have.

I am a marked man and may walk with a limp for the rest of my days here on earth, but I know it's good for me. It allows me to live out my next point.

2. Pull the plank and put it into perspective.

Listen to these sobering words from Jesus in Matthew 7:3-5 NKJV:

"And why do you look at the speck in your brother's eye, but do not consider the plank in your own eye? Or how can you say to your brother, 'Let me remove the speck from your eye'; and look, a plank is in your own eye? Hypocrite! First remove the plank from your own eye, and then you will see clearly to remove the speck from your brother's eye."

I have to first realize that I am not without fault or sin. I have blown it and made big time mistakes too. So instead of focusing on the speck in my dad's eye, I had to pull the big honking two by four out of my own eye! Then, I admit that I can't judge this man, only God can. When I pull the plank out of my own eye, it allows me to have the right perspective of this situation. God gives us a glimpse of what He sees about our life concerning our fathers. If your father hurt you, then God can use the pain he caused you to shape you to be who you are today. Perhaps you are saying, "I don't like who I am today. I don't like where I am in life."

"That's my point, Mike. That's why I can't forgive him because of what he did to me." Let me encourage you right here, because God is not done with you yet. In fact, I know that God will cause all things to work together in the grand scheme of things for your good in the end.

What makes great stories great? It's the great tragedies that are overcome and, my friend, if you will forgive, let go and let God work in you, He will turn your tragedy into triumph! Who I am today and the heart I have for my own children, and for all the millions of wounded sons and daughters, is because of what I went through. God will birth great ministry out of great misery! My perspective had to change before I could see change in this scenario. Once I did, then I can now be thankful for all the pain I went through because it is benefiting my children, my wife, my church and all those God uses me to touch for Him.

Forgiveness is not that you forget or say what you did was right. You relinquish your right to punish them. The devil wants to defeat you through this, and our great God wants to develop you through this betrayal. God uses betrayal for our benefit. Think about it. Where would Jesus be without Judas's kiss? Where would Joseph have been without his brothers pushing him into that pit? God used those betrayals to benefit these two lives and to carry them to their place of purpose in the Kingdom. I love what Joseph said when his brothers had betrayed him by pushing him into that pit some seventeen years earlier:

"But Joseph replied, 'Don't be afraid of me. Am I God, that I can punish you? You intended to harm me, but God intended it all for good. He

brought me to this position so I could save the lives of many people'" (Genesis 50:19,20).

Wow! Did you hear that Joseph, who had been pushed into a pit, sold into slavery, then sent to prison which ultimately led him to the king's palace said, *"Am I God, that I can punish you?"* He pulled the plank out and was able to put this thing into perspective. God used it to eventually help save the world from a famine. Lean in for a moment right here. God is going to use your pain to actually get you to your place of healing and blessing so that you can help save the lives of others. How amazing is that? Right? It's true! What happened to me was actually good for me in the end as God has used it and is using it now to impact the lives of people every single day of my life. He wants to do the same for you just like He did for Jesus, Joseph, me and countless others who have pulled the plank out of their own eye, extending grace and forgiveness to their offenders. You can do it! I know you can!

The last step is…

3. Pray for your offender(s).

This is exactly what God shows us to do for those who offend us, and that includes our fathers. He asks us to do it, and that's exactly what Jesus did on the cross. He was whipped, humiliated in public, hung on a cross, yet His perspective was clear through the bloody tears and excruciating pain of being executed by the very people He created and came to redeem. What amazing love! May we pull strength from the truth found in Luke 23:34: *"Jesus said, 'Father, forgive them, for they don't know what they are doing.'"*

Again, I want to point out the perspective we must keep in this: "They don't know." I contend that our fathers quite possibly couldn't have knowingly done what they did if they knew the devastating impact it would have on us. I am not saying that in some cases they didn't know, but I have to believe in my heart of hearts that somehow they were blinded by their own hurts and or blinded by the enemy. (See 2 Corinthians 4:4.)

God again echoes this principle of forgiveness and what our perspective and response should be to all who intentionally or unintentionally harm us: *"Bless those who curse you. Pray for those who hurt you"* (Luke 6:28).

Let me be the first to tell you from experience that PARTIAL FORGIVENESS WON'T DO IT! How do I know? Simple. When you speak of them or refer to them, is there anger, resentment or dishonor for them in your speech? I know that one indicator for me is that when I would share about my father, I knew I hadn't fully forgiven him because I wanted him to hurt. I wanted to dishonor his name and drag him through the mud of judgment when I would tell others what he had done.

If you say you have forgiven him and you recognize any of these attributes in your speech, it's a great indicator that you haven't forgiven in your heart. Jesus said in Matthew 12:34 NKJV, *"Out of the abundance of the heart the mouth speaks."* In other words, what comes out of our mouths reveals what is inside of our hearts.

God's will in this matter is clear. He loves you and forgives you. He wants to heal your heart, but you have to put the fence down. Pull the plank out so you can see the Lord Jesus on the cross looking at you, knowing that you have sinned and fallen short. Jesus is saying to the Father about you, "Forgive him for he knows not what he is doing." It's the same forgiveness that we receive from our gracious Savior that we, in turn, extend to our dads. Jesus said it was impossible that offences wouldn't come. They will happen. You will be whacked if you do and whacked if you don't! We can't control the offenses that happen to us, but we can control how we respond.

Who do you need to forgive? Forgive God? Forgive yourself? Forgive your dad? I want to encourage you to receive that forgiveness from God right now, and then extend it to those who need it. Say it out loud right now. If you can call them, then don't let another sun set until you do. If you can't contact them due to the fact that you have no idea where they are or they may be deceased, then write out their name on paper and say what you would if they were right there in front of you. If you can contact them, do it. I am confident you will be surprised at what happens.

I was approached by another gentleman who was my age or older who said recently in response to a message that he heard me speak that God told him to reach out to his dad. He did and he said he was fighting back fear of rejection. But that's not what he found. He found freedom in forgiving his dad, like a weight had been lifted off of him is the way he described it.

Are you carrying something that God never intended for you to carry? Give it to Jesus, because He carried it to the cross for you so that you don't have to carry it anymore.

The young lady I spoke of earlier, Karah, whose father had a stroke and was hospitalized, approached me after a worship service one Sunday with tears in her eyes. I knew she had been crying, but her countenance didn't look sad. She looked free. She told me that her father had passed away, but the Lord gave her and her brother a final moment with him where they were able to make amends. Forgiveness was given and restoration began for both of them. I believe it was by the love of Christ in them and because they decided to forgive just as

Jesus forgave them. Even the greatest offender who comes to Christ for forgiveness receives it unconditionally.

Isn't it time to say enough is enough? Make a decision today that you will not let this hurt from your father control your life any longer. You can have healing and freedom from your hurts today, so just say "yes" and the rest of your days can be the best of your days!

Why do we need to honor our fathers? Because it's the first decision that God ever made about your life. When you honor your earthly father, you are honoring your heavenly Father.

MEN UNWORTHY OF HONOR

As we wrap up this chapter, I want to conclude by helping you learn how to honor your father. "Are you serious?" you might ask. "How can I find the strength to forgive, and why should I honor my father?" I want to answer that and then offer a couple of practical steps to live it out.

First, I think it is important to know that when you honor your father, even if you think he is unworthy of honor, you will be honoring the perfect Father (God), who is absolutely worthy of ALL honor!

So what does the Bible say about how we are to treat fathers? Are there any conditions on which we are not to honor our fathers? I haven't found any in the Scriptures that give us conditions. It simply says this in Exodus 20:12: *"Honor your father...."*

This may seem crazy, but think about it like this. Your father was the first decision God made about your life. Again, you may be thinking, *That's exactly my problem with God.* I simply say, reread the first portion of this chapter to get the proper perspective. I wouldn't be who

I am today if God had given me another father. When I honor my father, I honor that decision that God made for my life that He created, designed and gave me in the first place.

Another reason is found in Ephesians 6:2-3: *"'Honor your father and mother' This is the first commandment with a promise. If you honor your father and mother 'things will go well for you, and you will have a long life on the earth.'"*

This is the only command of God's "big 10" that ends with a phenomenal promise. You will live long life, full of blessing. When you honor your father, whether he is worthy or not, you actually honor God and, in turn, God honors you with a long life full of blessing.

I love what I heard someone say once. They said that honor has a sound. There is a tone with honor. We can honor our fathers by the way we speak to them and the way we speak about them. Yes, it may take God's grace to do it, but with Christ we can do all things.

Begin to speak with a life-giving attitude to your father and watch what happens. Begin to speak with a tone of honor about your dad when you speak of him. A man's greatest need is for respect, and when you speak with honor to your father, you build up his sense of self-worth and his sense of respect. If he knows he is not worthy, it means all the more to him, and you are being the salt and light of Christ when you do.

Go ahead and give honor where it is due and even if you don't think it is due. I promise, it will make you better instead of bitter, blessed instead of stressed. God is pulling for you and so am I. I am praying for you because I know what God is doing in you.

The fact that you picked up this book and are reading it tells me that the Holy Spirit of God is leading your heart to a place of healing, forgiveness and freedom. I believe that restoration is beginning for you, so get ready! The best is yet to come!

CHAPTER 7

Let Restoration Begin

ONE OF MY favorite ways to spend my downtime is to watch movies. One of our favorite things to do as a family on Friday nights is to make something sweet to eat and watch a movie together. I really believe that movies are one of the modern ways God is speaking to us. Let's face it. Americans love movies.

It's amazing to me to see how many movies today are laced with the theme of fathers. As I have repeatedly said that as the Lord began to speak to me about this movement of healing fathers and their children, I started seeing it in multiple movies. For instance, the very well-known children's movie, "Finding Nemo." The movie depicts a father clown fish getting separated from his son, due in part to the son's disobedience and rebellion in going out into the deep. Nemo is captured by a diver, then scooped up in a boat that speeds away. In spite of the father's great fear of the unknown seas, his love for his only son drove him out of his comfort zone into dangerous waters to risk it all to find him. The story ends where he does find his son Nemo and their relationship is restored and is actually better in the end. This is just one of many films that spoke to me about the reality of fathers and their children.

This movie is a beautiful picture of what God wants for us as fathers and children: healing, forgiveness and restoration. He desires to see this as I do, and as I am sure you do too.

Destruction is the enemy's goal, but our God is greater and He prevails always. Restoration is God's goal, and this is what He is speaking through these conduits (movies) that move our souls.

WARRIOR

The modern-day warriors of our time are those who compete in MMA. It's definitely one of the more popular sports in our world today. Recently, the movie "Warrior" tells the story of two estranged brothers entering a mixed martial arts tournament, and deals with the brothers' struggling relationship with each other and with their father. The film opens with one son, Tommy, fresh out of the Marines, visiting his father, Paddy, a recovering alcoholic who has become a Christian. Tommy becomes angry about his father's formerly abusive behavior and Paddy fails to convince him that he has truly changed.

One thing that Tommy thought his dad could do right was train to fight. Tommy wants to win a MMA tournament, and though he wants his dad to train, he does not want to reconcile with him. Being a father who wants a second chance, Paddy agrees. Little do they know that the other son, Brendan, a former UFC fighter turned teacher, was going to enter as well for a chance to win the prize money for his struggling family.

Both sons were angry with their father, and they both had very good reasons to be. He was an abusive alcoholic who hurt them, their mother and their family. Years of warring within had now come to a head in all their lives. The father, Paddy, was seeking reconciliation, but like many children, the sons didn't want any part of it. The reason is not because they don't want reconciliation, but it is risking being hurt again by a father. That pain is so great that they are not willing to allow it to happen again. You may be like me in that I know exactly how they felt, but the result of this kind of thinking robs us of our inner peace.

There comes a time in the movie when Paddy was reaching out to Tommy and Tommy asks, "Where were you when it mattered most? I needed you then, but I don't need you now." Dad, that's true. We needed you then, but it's not true that we don't need you now. We needed you then and we need you now. We will always need you. It's a fundamental need of the human heart to desire the love, affection and approval of fathers in our lives as well as in the lives of our children.

Tommy unleashed his fury, vented his anger and rejected his dad. He thought that rejecting him would somehow fill the void and hurt in his heart, but it did not. You can't overcome evil with evil or rejection with rejection. When it comes to healing the father-child relationship, we must reconcile and bring the balance to zero, just as God the Father reconciled us through the Son.

Tommy went back to find his dad, who had been sober for years, drunk, crying and yelling. Paddy had given up and said, "What's the use?" and turns back to the bottle to drown his regrets. Tommy, seeing him like this, realized that it didn't bring fulfillment like he thought. The most powerful point in the movie to me is when Tommy walks towards his father, takes the liquor out of his hands and embraces his dad for the first time in who knows how long. It is here we see all the years of pain, war and hurt begin to break. Restoration began for Tommy and his dad that very moment. He was acknowledging his forgiveness and regrets. He, like many, has found the same to be true. If we reject those who have hurt us, especially our fathers, we are deceived into believing that it brings justice and makes things right, but it does not deliver!

Paddy would also go to reach out to his other son, Brendan, by being at the entrance of the aisle before every fight Brendan was about to compete in. Even as a grown man, I know that must have meant a lot to Brendan. He decided early on to forgive and reconcile the balance of the debt his father owed. Paddy as a dad wanted him to know – "I'm watching. Go win. Win, son." And that's what he did. He was the unlikely contender who won the battle. He had hurts and anger, but he was willing to forgive and reconcile. So if we want to win in life, we must do the same. In the end it was his love. Brendan won the tournament with his brother in his arms and Dad looking on with a smile. We all win when we surrender and tap out to God's love for us and then saying, "I love you, and I forgive you for what you did." Restoration begins in that very moment.

The only way to win is to follow Brendan's example. That way to victory is to forgive and reconcile, whether the father deserves it or not. You may feel like I did and like Tommy and Brendan did. All alone in the world without your dad, having to fight for everything. You have had to struggle, entering into adulthood because a father wasn't there to let you stand on his shoulders, showing you what to expect and teaching you how to prepare for what lies ahead. You have had to take your licks figuring it out as you go, many times through the sweat and tears, feeling abandoned at times.

This is exactly the way many of us have experienced life with our fathers. Perhaps you had a father, but you were estranged by some event or maybe you didn't have a father at all. Or maybe, like me, you had one, but you were without his presence at all in your life. Maybe you feel like you have been at war with your father externally or internally or both.

Has there been a lack of peace in your life? Have you felt as if you have built a fortress around your heart? Could it be that you don't have peace because of the war within yourself that is really a war with yourself? Where does this come from? Could it be exuding from the situations with your father or children that you have never dealt with? Let's take a look.

THE WAR WITHIN

So how do we settle the war within ourselves? How do we bring peace to this battle we have had concerning our fathers or our children? We can bring peace to this situation within, but we must first realize what Jesus came to do as the Son of the Father. He came to us when we were far away from God to make peace between God and ourselves. Ephesians 2:12-14 says, *"You lived in this world without God and without hope. But now you have been united with Christ Jesus. Once you were far away from God, but now you have been brought near to him through the blood of Christ. For Christ himself has brought peace to us. He united Jews and Gentiles into one people when, in his own body on the cross, he broke down the wall of hostility that separated us."*

This was Jesus' mission. This is what He does in us. If we have asked Him to come into our lives and given Him our hearts, then we can have peace, because that's what He does. So if we don't have peace, then it means this area of our life has not been submitted to Him.

Here are a few truths that will bring peace and settle the war within your own life and your situation.

1. You won't find peace until you <u>make peace</u>.

You can't settle your issues with self without settling the issues with others. People today – even Christians – think it's okay to not settle it, and Scriptures teach us that it's not. They can be led to believe that *because they think they are right* God says, "That's earthly thinking." James 3:17-18 NIV says, *"But the wisdom that comes from heaven is first of all pure; then <u>peace-loving</u>, considerate, submissive, full of mercy and good fruit, impartial and sincere. Peacemakers who sow in peace raise a harvest of righteousness."*

The result of peacemaking is righteousness. They are connected. Peacemaking brings righteousness and likewise righteousness brings peace. The way you and I make peace is by bringing righteousness into the situation. In this case, forgiveness and reconciliation is the standard. Bring the righteous standard of God into the situation and you will bring in God's supernatural power with it. You will not have peace if you violate God's principles. But if you bring God's standard into this relationship or any relationship for that matter, you will have peace that you have always wanted and hoped for. Being a peacemaker brings happiness to our lives. It brings a blessing with it just like Jesus said in Matthew 5:9 NKJV: *"Blessed are the peacemakers, for they shall be called sons of God."* The word "blessed" here when translated in some places is "happy" – happiness that goes beyond circumstances – not external, but rather an internal joy that we can have when we choose to be peacemakers. You will not find peace until you make peace. So how do you make peace?

2. You make peace through <u>reconciliation</u>.

Peace comes through this powerful truth that I hope you can download into the hard drive of your spirit. This is what many know to do, but so many don't want to do it, and they never find peace. To understand this more clearly, think of it like this: To reconcile means to bring the balance to a zero. If you are diligent with your finances, you know that you are supposed to reconcile your bank statement every month. Simply put, you crunch all the numbers and hope to bring the balance to a zero.

It is the same with making peace between fathers and children. You forgive them of their debt by bringing the balance to zero. You may have said within yourself, "You owe me for what you did," or "you are going to pay for what you did." What we are really saying is, "You have a debt that you will pay to me one way or another." To make peace, through the mercy and heart of Christ, we need only to bring the balance to a zero. In fact, Jesus, just a few breaths later, said how happy peacemakers would be and that they are so much like God that people would call them God's children. We hear Him saying this in Matthew 5:23-24 NKJV: *"Therefore if you bring your gift to the altar, and there remember that your brother has something against you, leave your gift there before the altar, and go your way. First be reconciled to your brother, and then come and offer your gift."*

God is showing us how important reconciliation is to Him and to us, because He wants us to have peace. Peace is vital to us living the happy life He desires for us all. If you want to know how to overcome the inner war and conflict, this is how it is done. Conflict resolution rarely works, because God doesn't say to resolve conflict. He says we are to reconcile conflict. In fact, you can't have resolve until you have reconciliation.

Let me explain to you what I mean. Remember, Jesus didn't come to *resolve* our sin – He *reconciled* it. We owed a huge debt to Him for our sins, which were many. Yet He still laid down His life, shed His blood to forgive our debts and reconcile us, or in other words, He brought our balance to a zero. Second Corinthians 5:19 NKJV says, *"God was in Christ reconciling the world to Himself, not imputing their trespasses to them, and has committed to us the word of reconciliation."* God the Father reconciled you and me so that we could also reconcile with not only God, but with others as well. This includes our fathers. God wants us to bring their balance to a zero and we will have peace. We will settle the war within. I know it's hard, you may not want to and some of you reading this right now are thinking, *You are asking the impossible.* But, my friend, you have to trust the principles of God's Word. It really works! If you will work God's Word, it will work for you too. Lastly...

3. You can't reconcile until you have been <u>reconciled</u>.

You and I must be reconciled to God first; then that love gives us the capacity to love with the God-kind of love: unconditional. If you will bring Jesus into this situation, Who is righteousness, you will have peace. But you first need to bring Him into your heart and life. When you do, a miracle takes place. God will do the supernatural as you spend time with Him in prayer, and sometimes it takes fasting for breakthrough in our own hearts to see through the precious love of heaven that Jesus has for us and for them!

STORIES OF RESTORATION

On December 13, 2009, I had a great breakthrough with my mother. She didn't want to admit that she had a father wound, even though I knew that she did. Her memories of her father were ones filled with abuse and alcohol. Abuse towards her mother, but not so much toward her. But I know that he left my mother and her family when she was very young. There has been a father void missing in her life for a long time, but God is healing her in this area. It is interesting as to how He was leading me to contribute to this process.

So for her fifty-ninth birthday, I contacted her father to set up a surprise lunch with her. Now you must understand that my grandfather, who is still alive and within driving distance of me and my mom, doesn't reach out to us at all. However, I was glad to be able to initiate this meeting because it gave me time for something I have never really had with him, face-to-face. I was able to spend some time with him. I have only been in his presence maybe three times that I can recall in my entire life.

As we had the chance to talk alone at the table, waiting for my mother to come, I was extremely inquisitive. After hearing his story about his father, it made sense to me why at one time in his past life he was an abusive alcoholic. When I asked him about his father, he informed me that he was a quiet man who didn't say much, but would beat him till he bled if he didn't act according to his rules. He said he left home angry when he was fifteen to go to work and make his way in life. That is not the way to launch out into manhood, too early, too hurt and too angry. The dots were really connecting for me now.

He also told me about his encounter with God and how, while detoxing in a hospital, he felt the room get very hot and his bed stood vertically. As he looked down, he said he could see hell. The Lord asked him if he wanted to live, and he said "yes," then gave his heart to Christ and has been sober ever since. Nevertheless, he still didn't know very much about being a good father. In my quest to be a good father, I knew I needed to set these two up for some healing to take place.

Anyone who knows my mother will tell you that she is hard to surprise, but I have to say that this day she had no idea who would be sitting at the table with me. I will never forget the look on her face when she walked in, I positioned myself strategically so that I could see her face and she couldn't see her father's. It was clear to me that she was pleasantly surprised. I could see it in her face how much it meant to her.

Knowing that my mom's love language is gift giving, I handpicked a birthday card and was going to ask him to sign it to give to her. I didn't want to risk something like this to cause more disappointment by not being considerate enough to buy a card, but to my delight, he also prepared a card for her that he brought himself. I took a couple of snapshots as we had experienced something there for the very first time ever. There we were – me, my mom and her dad – celebrating her. I am not sure if she had ever experienced this or even if she realized the weight of what I was trying to give to her. I would like to believe that she did.

During our time there, he did the best he could to show love to her. I have to believe that it was a day that restoration went into motion for her and him.

Another gentleman in my church, who is in his fifties, shared a story with me recently about his own father. He had not spoken with his dad for several years since the death of his mother. The father was angry and withdrew from all the kids only to remarry and move on. My friend went on to say that during a message I was sharing one Sunday, it inspired him to take the initiative to make amends with his father.

So one day he jumped on his Harley and headed to Florida uninvited. He said that when he was a few miles away, he called to inform his father of his close proximity and his desire to pop in. The surprised father said, "Of course, come on by." My friend John went on to tell me that when he pulled up in the driveway that his father was there with tears in his eyes, waiting for him to arrive. The two of them embraced and exchanged loving words that instantly reconciled their relationship where they stood. Just like that. John had a choice. He could have prayed about it for a couple of more days, weeks or months, but instead he acted on what he knew God was leading him to do.

You can do that too. If you have the chance, maybe you need to jump on a Harley or an airplane and go where your father is. Maybe you should get on the phone today or write a letter to him to let restoration begin. If you can't because you don't know where he is or he may not be alive in this world any longer, you can still express your heart even though you can't get to him. Write it down, call out his name, get it out of your heart in whatever manner works best for you, but do it. Release and watch restoration begin for you too.

I walked through this, and you need to know that God can restore your relationship with your father. The enemy stole my relationship with my dad as a boy, but then as I turned to God for healing and I extended that to my father, it released the restoration process for us. Not only did God restore it, He allowed me to baptize my dad and also gave me an incredible stepdad who helped me plant our church. He is still serving today. He also gave me a great father-in-law who also helped plant our church and is still an active part of my life. God didn't stop there. He has given me two great spiritual fathers who love me and coach me to this day.

God wants your story to end well. If you have had a painful life story, God doesn't want it to end that way. He wants you to have a new beginning. He wants to begin a new chapter of healing and restoration. There is no limit to what God can do when you bring Him into your situation! God sent His Son and risked it all because of His love for you. God gave His Son because He wants you as His child. That's the greatest story ever told. It can be your story. All you have to do is turn to Him, call upon Him and ask Him to be your Savior, healer and redeemer.

Look at this wonderful promise in 2 Corinthians 6:18 NKJV where God says, *"I will be a Father to you, and you shall be My sons and daughters, says the Lord Almighty."* "I will be a Father to you," God says, "if you will come out from among this world and reach out for Me."

My friend, you hold the power to begin that process. You can hold on to your bitterness and let it spoil your life and the lives of those around you that you love and care about, like Tommy from the movie "Warrior," or you can swallow your pride, and in the midst of your pain, reach out to forgive so that restoration can begin. In fact, like a car being restored, it will be more valuable than it was originally, because it came at a higher price. It costs more humility, love and mercy.

God the Father's heart has turned to us as wayward sons and daughters. He has reconciled us back to Himself through Jesus Christ. When a father turns to his children, something powerful and miraculous happens. So Dad, if that speaks to you, turn your heart to God right now for forgiveness and He will give you grace for your guilt, unforgiveness and failures. Then, turn your heart to your child or children today while you have the chance. It's never too late, and if at first they don't receive you because they are hurting and angry, don't give up. Keep reaching out and show them that they are worth fighting for. Fight for them, fight for their heart. It may take several rounds, but make up your mind that nothing can stop you and you will be the last man standing.

If this speaks to you as a son or a daughter and you are able to reconcile, then do it. I know how that feels to battle abandonment, rejection and anger. But learn from my story and even from Tommy who lashed out at his dad, thinking it would heal that wound or make peace, but it won't. IT WON'T! Evil cannot conquer evil, but you can overcome evil with good.

You can overcome through Jesus Christ. We must receive that love and forgiveness, be reconciled back to God and let Him bring your balance to a zero. Then you can have the ability to do the same with your father. I promise you, you will be glad that you did. God wants restoration to begin, and I am praying for you that you will do just that. God will cause your latter days to be better than your beginning. You can be the champion God wants you to be. If you will trust in Him, I know He will do what He said He would do. He is a good God, so expect His goodness to come your way as you let restoration begin.

CHAPTER 8

Generational Momentum

ARCHIE MANNING PLAYED quarterback for the New Orleans Saints long before Drew Brees helped bring a Super Bowl championship to the city. Archie, a very talented quarterback who had set SEC records in college at the University of Mississippi, never won a championship game. In the NFL, it was even worse as he played for the Saints for ten seasons. Nine of them were losing while only once getting to a five hundred average season. By the end of his career, his record as a starter was 35–101–3 (26.3%), the worst in NFL history among quarterbacks with at least 100 starts.

This highly skilled ball player never knew what it was like to win it all and play in the big game. However, as we talk about what God is doing in restoring fathers and their children, I want you to notice how God is showing us through the number one sport in America. Archie has three boys, and two of them went on to play college football, and you guessed it, as quarterbacks. These two boys hung around their father while watching his faithfulness to Christ. Their mother and football had begun to rise upon the generational momentum. Yes, the download of Daddy all the way to the pros. Can you imagine having not only one but two sons make it to the professional level of their craft?

Oh, it gets better. As if that wasn't amazing enough, think about this. The oldest son is Peyton Manning, current quarterback of the Indianapolis Colts. He took his team to Super Bowl XLI in 2007 and won. Wow! What a day of honor and celebration for this family who never tasted victory before and now to do it through their son's lifetime. You would think that was the pinnacle, but check this out and think about how the very next season his youngest son, Eli Manning, took his New York Giants as quarterback to play against an 18-0 red hot New England Patriots and won! Are you kidding me? One dad with no Super Bowl appearances, and then through generational blessing and momentum, not one but two sons win back-to-back Super Bowls!

It is evident that God is speaking loud and clear to American men about His plans to restore the generational blessing to those who will receive it. As one who watched football for over thirty-five years, played football for ten years of my life and now coach Little League for my boys over the last five years, I have been blown away by what I have witnessed through the story of Archie Manning and his two sons, Peyton and Eli. God is projecting what He is doing, saying, "This is what I am doing in this country and even in this world. I am restoring the generational blessing. I am speaking to all the dads out there, all the sons, all the daughters. I am going to turn hearts toward Me, because I am the God of *Abraham, Isaac and Jacob!* God is the God of generational blessing and momentum so that the next generation can go further faster!

That is what generational momentum is all about. Those coming after us should be able to stand on our shoulders and see further, sooner and go higher than we ever could. That's God's plan, that's God's idea! Satan, the enemy of our souls, knows that and that is why he has tried to disrupt ever since the garden, when God told him that the generation coming from Adam would one day crush his head (Genesis 3).

It comes down from the father – curse or blessing. What are you sending down? Dr. Dale C. Bronner, who is a spiritual father in my life, has billboards all over the west side of Atlanta. They read, "What legacy will you leave?" Carey Casey, the CEO for National Fathering Center and author of *Championship Fathering*, wrote about the difference between heritage and legacy. He teaches that heritage is what is handed to you by your fathers. We don't have any control over what is handed to us. Legacy, on the other hand, is what you leave for your children. When it comes to heritage, we have no choice, but with legacy we do. If we aren't proud of the heritage that was handed to us, then we can work towards leaving a legacy that we are proud of. Unlike Casey, who had a great heritage handed to him, which is God's way, unfortunately I did not. I wasn't proud of the heritage handed to me, if you want to call it that. I am not bitter about it. I took a look at the family tree. There wasn't a heritage passed to my father or to his father. Now, as a follower of Jesus Christ and through the grace of God, I am learning how to be a great father so that I can leave a legacy that not only I, but my children, are proud of.

Every good gift comes down from the father (James 1:17). God intended you to be a conduit of blessing, sending good gifts and only good gifts down to the generations that follow you. I know that you are probably like me in the sense that you definitely want to pass down as much good as you can to your children, who are not only your children but your grandchildren's parents!

In the Bible, we see a momentum that is released from one generation to the next. I believe it is and always has been God's desire to see positive momentum of heritage passed down from father to children/son. I think about Abraham, known as the father of faith, had a son, Isaac, who eventually had a son named Jacob. God is known throughout history as the God of Abraham, Isaac and Jacob.

The generational momentum God desires is a powerful force that will grow from one generation to the next, helping them to go further faster. Abraham had two sons, but God's son of promise was Isaac. Isaac had two sons, one being Jacob. By the time we get to Jacob, he has a whopping twelve sons. This is actually where the twelve tribes of Israel came from which today has become the nation of Israel. God took one man and made him a father of many nations.

God wants us to receive generational momentum from those who have come before us so that we can take it to greater levels for His glory. There is a force of blessing released when fathers lay their hands on their sons and daughters to bless them as seen with Abraham, Isaac and Jacob. This reminded me of a statement I once heard Zig Ziglar say: "Out of forty thousand prisoners in Florida, only thirteen were Jewish due in large part to the fact that Jewish fathers lay their hands on their sons like Abraham did, telling them that they love them and bless them."

When fathers live in such a way as to honor the heavenly Father, it releases some powerful stuff into the ones coming after them. I see this lived out today in churches across America. There are so many examples of this today to confirm what I am saying. I think about Joel Osteen. Joel pastors one of the largest churches in America today and has multiple books he has written on the New York Times best seller's list. You may not know it, but his father, John Osteen who founded the church, was a great man of God and a great father. He passed down some incredible generational momentum to Joel, and because of the blessing passed down, Joel has gone further faster.

It took his father years to see the church grow to 6,000 members, which is a great achievement, and he wrote several great books. When John died, he looked to Joel to carry the torch. He received his father's blessing and has seen the church grow to nearly 45,000 in a few short years.

I am amazed at how people see this and they want to criticize the success or discredit his ministry, but I think it is important to understand that Joel was chosen by God and confirmed by his father, John, so he has downloaded the power of God's generational blessing. I salute the Osteen family, and I am still encouraged by their ministry today as I was when Pastor John was preaching every week. It still blesses me when I see how much Joel's father impacted him that even after years of going on to be with the Lord. Joel gets choked up and teary-eyed every time he refers to his father.

Recently, I had an opportunity to fly to Houston to meet with Joel and the entire Osteen family. It was such an amazing experience for my wife and me. Joel invited about seventy pastors of life-giving, like-minded churches that are about loving God and loving people. One thing I took away was the fact that physics teaches a law, which says, the lower an object is to the ground the faster it can go. What my wife and I experienced was great love and humility, which told me a lot of why God has raised up Joel for God's glory. Joel, his brother, sister and mother told the Lakewood story which in itself is totally amazing. I was so touched to think of the mark that their father and husband had made on their lives.

They said he taught them to always have sweet words, because you will never know how many you will have to eat. Even at this level of success, they were teary-eyed, smiling and pouring out love to us. John Osteen downloaded Jesus to his children, and now they are all in ministry, overseeing a ministry of over 40,000 people attending every week, that has 20 million viewers on television every month and "Night of Hope" meetings all over the world.

In one night in Yankee stadium, twenty-five thousand stood up to receive Christ! What a legacy John Osteen downloaded to his children and to his children's children. He may not have had a great heritage given to him by the generation before, but through Jesus Christ he was able to download a legacy that is still making a mark on the world, including me.

Now you may be thinking, *Well, if my dad had been like that, I could do something significant too.* Don't think like that. You may be like me in that I wasn't handed any heritage at all. My dad worked in the transportation industry. He didn't have any generational blessing momentum passed down to him. But now through redemption in Jesus Christ, as a seed of father Abraham, I can receive the same blessing God had on him. Now I am able to be the one God uses to start the generational blessing momentum for the generation coming after me.

My prayer is that my children will be even better and go further faster in their lifetime. John Osteen was just a popcorn salesman who was saved by the grace of God. Then he decided he was going to reach his potential and not complain about what he didn't have. If God did it with John and if He is doing it for me, then, my friend, He is willing to do it for you if you are willing.

Like it or not, Joel has the power of God's generational blessing working for him. Instead of criticizing and questioning the validity of his ministry, maybe we should be seeking to find out more about how we too can download and establish this generational blessing for us and our children. Maybe we should download a spirit that celebrates anyone who is pointing people to Christ and bringing multitudes closer to Jesus.

As I said earlier, there are many great stories out there about people you may or may not have heard of: Charles and Andy Stanley, Ed Young Sr. and Ed Young Jr., Larry and Joel and Jonathan Stockstill, Tommy and Matthew Barnett, Billy and Jentezen Franklin, and then Wendall and Judah Smith, as well.

I am so encouraged to see the beauty of God's power released in the generational transfer that is allowing these second and third generation pastors to go further faster than those who came before them.

Maybe you are like me and you didn't have a heritage handed to you like these great dads handed to their children. Don't have a pity party or get discouraged, saying, "Not fair," because if God is your Father, you can still do some amazing things in your lifetime.

Look at David, a shepherd who was not acknowledged by his father when the prophet Samuel showed up. That didn't stop him, He kept on worshipping and serving his Father in heaven and he became a first generation king!

Again, remember that some of these men who have seen the blessing momentum grow stronger in their children's lives and have left a great legacy and handed down a remarkable heritage, didn't have a great heritage either. But through God's love, grace and favor they have accomplished phenomenal feats as well as downloaded this powerful, God-giving generational blessing. God has no favorites. If these men did it, so can we with faith and perseverance.

WHAT ABOUT MAMA?

To all the moms who are reading this chapter, I believe God is speaking to you in regard to this as well. What are you supposed to do if your child doesn't have a godly father in his life, or what if his dad isn't a believer? I want to encourage you today. There are many moms who are raising their children without the active assistance of their children's fathers. Single moms and moms who might as well be single moms, did you know that over 20 million American kids are being raised by their single moms?

Let's look at a young, single mom named Eunice. Eunice grew up in a household of faith. Her mother, Lois, was a deeply spiritual woman. Eunice loved all the Bible stories. She probably went to services every time the doors were open. But when Eunice was a teenager, she gave her heart to a young man who wasn't of the same faith nor was he Jewish. He didn't feel the same about spiritual matters as she did. And probably against the advice of her mother, Eunice married the young man and had a baby. Eunice named her baby Timothy. What's really interesting about that name is that Timothy's name means "one who honors God."

Not long after Timothy was born, Timothy's daddy died. Eunice found herself responsible for raising her child as a single mom. She realized she needed some help, so she invited her mother, Lois, to move in with them to help her raise little Timothy.

I would imagine that Eunice and Lois spent hours with Timothy telling him Bible stories, teaching him about God, shaping his heart, mind, life and character through God's Word.

Then, a man named Paul came through their hometown of Lystra. As usual Paul shared the gospel of Jesus Christ in that town with everyone. Perhaps in one particular meeting Eunice and Lois soon realized that what Paul said made sense, and they put their faith in Jesus.

Timothy, now a teenager, made the same choice by accepting Christ and placing his faith in Him. Paul met Timothy and took a great interest in Timothy. Paul invited Timothy to join him in his missionary travels. Timothy became Paul's right-hand man. Paul became his spiritual father and referred to Timothy as a true son in the faith. Eventually, Timothy became the pastor of one of the great early churches, the church at Ephesus. Wow! How's that for generational momentum and blessing? First, it started with Lois, then she passed it down to Eunice and they passed it on to Timothy who became Paul's right-hand man and a great pastor whose heritage was recorded in the Bible!

I also am amazed about what a mother can do to pass down generational momentum. I think about the story of world-renowned recording artist Israel Houghton. He was born to a single mother who had been rejected by her family at seventeen because she was pregnant and not married. But it also was because of the fact it was from an interracial relationship, his mother Caucasian and his father Jamaican. His mother later became a Christian and encouraged Israel's faith in Christ, and he has accomplished great things. Not only is he accomplishing great things in his lifetime, he is establishing a legacy for his children and will certainly pass down the generational blessing to help them go further faster.

You must understand that this is what God planned from the start, and He is now restoring this amazing truth to us who will simply believe it and be available to Him to generate it. How? I speak to that in another chapter, but it simply starts by us having a genuine, authentic faith that we first live out and then pass on to our children through intentional discipleship, teaching them the Word of God, prayer, worship, serving and giving in the local church.

Just sell out to Christ and live a life fully surrendered to Him is the foundation for passing down that generational blessing momentum for those coming behind you. Dads, you are constantly teaching your child through your words, actions and attitudes. It is called modeling, and the good news is that they model the positive things you project, but the bad news is that they model the negative things you project as well. This is why we must rely daily upon our love walk with our heavenly Father.

I know that I can't be the father He wants me to be and they need me to be without spending time with the Perfect Father. It's here that I can see what He is like, then model His nature and character. Jesus, the Son, said in John 5:19, *"I tell you the truth, the Son can do nothing by himself. He does only what he sees the Father doing. Whatever the Father does, the Son also does."*

You see, Dad, this is why it is so important to be a son first. If I am going to succeed as a father, husband, pastor, leader and friend, I must spend time with my heavenly Father as much as I can. Everything good that flows from my life to others is directly connected from my relationship with God as His child first and foremost. That is the core of passing down the generational blessing God wants to channel through you so that your children can go further faster than you ever imagined.

IT GOES BOTH WAYS

The devil understands this Kingdom principle and that is why he targets men, especially fathers, so that he can disrupt this powerful force that God wants us to use for good. Make no mistake; Satan will target women too in this matter. Whomever he can devour, he will.

Think about how Adam was made in the image of God, yet when he sinned in the Garden, he played the blame game refusing to take responsibility for his sin, saying, "It's that woman You gave me." His sin was passed down to his son, Cain, who ended up killing his brother. When God asked him about it, he said, *"Am I my brother's keeper?"* (Genesis 4:9 NKJV). In other words, I am not responsible for that sin.

It's amazing how this negative generational momentum was released at such a rate that only a few short chapters later we see the earth filled with so much wickedness that God said He was sorry he made people. He ended up erasing the people He created for blessing.

I submit that it started in a man, a father no less, who sinned and passed it on to his son, who in turn did the same. Also, notice that when God wanted to start over, He found a man, a father named Noah, who took his sons along with their wives who would obey God by building an ark. God starts over with Noah, also a father, along with his three sons, and God said, *"Be fruitful and multiply."* Noah obeyed God and released the generational blessing back into the earth once again, and from these three sons came the human race as we know it.

Exodus 20:5 says, *"I lay the sins of the parents upon their children; the entire family is affected – even children in the third and fourth generations of those who reject me."* Sins of the fathers are passed down to the third and fourth generation. That is pretty heavy stuff. After giving my life to Christ in my mid twenties, I heard a profound teaching from God's Word that explained a lot and answered a lot of questions for me, like, "Why me? Why did I mess up so much time and time again? Why did I feel cursed?" Because I was cursed according to Exodus 20.

Now, when I talk about this, you have one or two directions you can go. First, you can say, "Hey, that's just wrong and not fair at all. I am a victim and I am not responsible for my rebellious, self-serving lifestyle." Or you can say, "Hey, that's just the way it is. It was out of my control and maybe it doesn't seem fair, but that's just the way it is." For me, I battled those feelings and the devil was trying to get me into bitterness, which rots your soul in the long run. That's not a good thing.

God in His love gave me a proper perspective in the matter. As I began to look up my family tree, I could see three or four generations up the tree. My fathers had blown it big time. Now, I am not judging them or pointing the finger at them and neither should you. More than likely they had downloaded the momentum of generational cursing. That's right, generational cursing. It is biblical and we can see this in the New Testament as well as in the Old. Matthew 27:25 shows us that they were about to crucify Jesus and *"All the people answered, 'Let his blood be on us and on our children!'"* (NIV).

This is why when I speak to students and adults, I try to convey the seriousness of the decisions we make. Whenever we make a decision as teens, young or fully grown, our decisions don't just affect us, but those who are coming after us, the generations that are within us still in seed form.

Generational curses gain momentum as well. Take Abraham, for example. Though he was considered the father of faith and the friend of God, he made a bad decision that shows up in the next generation, and by the third generation, we see it multiplied.

Abram was passing through a country and told his wife, Sarai, to say that she was his sister if asked by the men so that they would not kill him to get her. The truth is that she was his half sister, and he was only twisting the truth a little. Right? Well, to be truth, it has to be 100 percent true; 99 percent doesn't qualify as truth.

They encounter a king and Sarai lies and says that Abram is her brother. Then we see his son, Isaac, does the same thing and the stories are identical. When Isaac, who was second generation, has children, he has twins. One of them is given the name Jacob, which in Hebrew means trickster, and trickster he was. He tricked his own father by posing as his older brother, Esau, to steal the firstborn blessing. Again, we see this showing up in Jacob's life when his own sons sell Jacob's favorite son, Joseph, into slavery. They lied to Jacob and the curse goes on.

What started four generations previous to this is a man telling one seemingly small lie. By the time it hits the fourth generation, we see a father agonizing over the alleged death of his favorite son. It is clear to see how one decision to lie was downloaded and gained momentum by the time it reached the fourth generation.

Make no mistake, God isn't glad when that happens. I don't believe He delights in that for us. I believe He delights in seeing the blessing expand and gain momentum from one generation to the next.

I began to look up my family tree and noticed divorce, alcoholism, adultery, fear, depression and an extreme lack of fatherlessness. My mother's father was an adulterous, abusive alcoholic who left my grandmother with six children, while my mother was still a child. My father's father was not an alcoholic, but from my father's perspective he was emotionally absent, so basically he was fatherless emotionally. When my father was in his first year of college, his parents divorced and it affected him to the point that he dropped out. Although my father's father was not an alcoholic, his mother was. He too would eventually fall prey to alcoholism and infidelity.

My father struggles with expressing his emotions to me today, I believe due largely to the download he received from his own father. Empathy is a characteristic that I would use to describe my father, and it was being downloaded to me. I struggled as well with empathy and expressing my emotions. Worse than that, I had destructive addictions. They struggled with alcohol, and now the curse momentum hit my life that propelled me to go deeper into addictions. I not only was addicted to alcohol, I was addicted to marijuana, meta amphetamines, ecstasy and cocaine. I too began ripping through relationships and sexual one-night stands at a rate far greater than my fathers before me.

My life was headed downhill in the dark at 110 miles per hour. This was a picture of what negative generational momentum looks like. I was not only on the same track as my father, I was doing more damage to myself and to others at a faster rate. I was going further faster in the wrong direction. I was headed to the grave at a more rapid rate than those who passed down the negative momentum before me because that is how it works, good or bad.

In essence, ladies and gentlemen, we carry a lot of generational opportunity to pass down a heritage that is full of blessing and power to succeed in life or self-destruct in a hurry! Regardless of where you are today, you can make a positive change for the future generations that will come forth from you. It doesn't matter what heritage was handed to you through the cross of Christ, you can reverse the curse into a blessing.

Back to our scripture in Exodus on sins being passed down to the third and fourth generation, I know you may have felt that is was totally unfair of a loving God to do that. If God chose my parents, then He must not love me very much. You are wrong. God loves deeply, consistently and unconditionally. He doesn't love you randomly or by how you should be or could be, but He loves you just as you are. It bothered Him so much that we were living under a curse, He sent His firstborn Son Jesus Christ to shed His pure blood, die and rise from the dead to break the power of the curse from your life so that you could experience the blessed life no matter what side of the tracks you were born on.

REVERSE THE CURSE

I want you to also notice in Galatians 3:13, it says that Jesus Christ became a curse and literally consumed the generational curse by hanging on the cross, not only to have our sins removed, but also to have the generational blessing released upon us. The blessing that was on Abraham can come upon us who turn to Christ and trust Him by giving our lives to follow Him. Though out of our control, sins may have been passed down to us, but God provided His own Son, Jesus, to absorb those sins, so that He could restore and release His generational blessing upon our life. God is a good God and the best Father in the universe. He doesn't glory in generational curses, but in blessing. God is a giver, not a taker. However, He has given us the power to choose between life and death, blessing and cursing. He says, "Choose life" so it will go well with us and our children.

As bad as the negative momentum that was passed down to me was, through the cross of Christ, the curse has been reversed. I now have been entrusted with three beautiful children who are enjoying God's generational blessing. I am releasing my faith and imparting blessing to them. I labor daily to do all I can to ensure that they receive a godly heritage that they can launch from.

Psalm 27 says that children are like arrows in the hand of a warrior. In crafting arrows, it is essential that the arrowhead be shaped correctly with precision. As a father, I am called to shape my children like arrows, aim their lives toward their destiny so that they hit the mark, going further faster. I know that they will go further faster in the right direction because of God's amazing grace upon my life. It's not an easy work, but it's an extremely important work that brings rewards for generations to come.

ANSWER THE CALL

Take Tamar, the father of Abraham, who lost a son and it caused him a lot of pain. Perhaps if he had gone on from the land of Ur, he would have been the father of faith. He never could leave the place of pain where his son died, so could it have been recorded in Scriptures as the God of Tamar, Abraham and Isaac? Instead, it became his son and grandsons – Abraham, Isaac and Jacob.

My mom told me that my father felt called to ministry as a young twenty something, but for whatever reason, he did not fully answer that call. I can't help but think that God wanted to use my father as a first generation pastor, and I was going to be second instead of first. It's neither here nor there, because he may not have had the opportunities I did in my church with the leadership God put me under. However, I think it is interesting to note the truth that God wants to start with you, Dad, with you, Mom, right now. He wants you to be the first or to continue to pass it down, but you have to see yourself as God sees you so that you can do what He has called you to do.

Dad, Mom, if you don't answer the call of God in your life, God will look to your children. So will the enemy of our souls, Satan. But our God is faithful and if we will commit our lives to Him, trusting Him, fully devoted to Him, He will make sure His plan for you will come to pass. God promises that when we are in covenant with Him, He will not allow the enemy to rob us of our children ever again! Ezekiel 36:12 states it clearly, *"You will never again rob them of their children."*

I believe God is calling you to be that link to bridge God's generational blessing to the third and fourth generation, that your children will go further faster and reach their potential, fulfilling God's will in their generation for His glory! They will hit the target God marked out for them before He created the world. God is using you to change the world! Get ready, for your best days are still in front of you and you will see the goodness of the Lord in the land of the living.

CHAPTER 9

A Father's Touch

TOUCH IS A powerful expression and necessity that we all need to develop from the time we come from the womb until the day we leave this world. It's a fact that infants need human touch or they could actually die. Clinical studies have shown that infants' emotional and physical health is directly connected to the level of touch they receive, especially in the first year of life. Another study that was done with nearly seven thousand fathers and their children over the course of a few years showed that a father's touch actually impacted the child's cognitive development for the good. It went on to say that dads who touch their children often through hugs and kisses actually produced happier, healthier children emotionally and physically.

We need the touch of fathers in our lives. That's the way God created us to be. When children are born, they have an instinctive desire to be touched. As I said before, when they are not held, comforted or rocked, they will not develop properly in many ways. My wife saw this firsthand when she went to Russia on a mission trip as they visited local orphanages. She recalls that it broke her heart to see these abandoned children rocking themselves back and forth due to the absence of touch within the early years of development. The people operating the orphanages explained to them the theory for their rocking.

I have heard that in certain native tribal cultures, the first person to hold a child fresh from the womb was not a female nurse or a doctor, but rather, the child's father before anyone else. They believe it is imperative to have Dad be the first hands the child felt.

I have been so very blessed to have had the glorious experience of childbirth three times with my sons Michael Jr., Presley and my daughter Madelyn. Upon learning this about the fathers being first to touch, I was the first person, other than the doctor and nurse, to hold all three of my children when they were born. I even went to the extent of touching them way before they were breathing oxygen in this world. I would lay hands on Charla's belly and sing to them, pray over them and speak God's Word to them.

For dads of infants and dads to be, I highly recommend that you do it too. It has been very instrumental in my deep connection with all three of my children. I learned the importance of feeding them their bottle, and experts even taught that touching skin by the father was extremely important. The power of touch, the power of a father's touch, is very needed in babies but also as we grow into adults too.

Dad, whatever your child's age, they need your embrace and touch still. I know it may feel awkward because they are not small anymore, but take it from a man who needed that touch that it does matter. No matter what our age, our father's embrace represents security for us, even when we are full grown, hairy legged men! That goes for women as well. Dad, you will always be a very important man in her life and she still wants your touch in her life.

Not only do we need physical touch for healthier, happier children, I contend that we need a father's touch spiritually as well. I will offer some ways that you can do that later in this chapter.

You may be saying, "How can I know with certainty this is true? I mean, Mike, I didn't have a father's touch and I am doing just fine." I am going to use my own life to speak to it and maybe it will help. You may be all right. I thought I was too until I was touched by the Father God, I didn't realize that's what I longed for in this world. I didn't realize how much I needed a father's touch until I was in my mid twenties. I didn't know what it was like to have a man, a father, speaking into my life, touching my potential to be something great for God. I had not been crowned as a man, I was still a boy in many ways who needed a father to validate me, love me and even rebuke me.

It all begins first and foremost with God the Father's tender touch in our lives. When God the Father touches us, it causes us to be healed. It causes us to grow, multiply and fulfill our potential. God uses the touch of our natural and spiritual fathers to actually accomplish this through them for us, and then through us as fathers who are fathers.

FATHER FOUNDATION

A father's touch is so important in so many ways. Fathers have always been used in establishing foundational things, starting with the heavens and the earth, founded by our Father in heaven (See Hebrews 11:3). This includes Abraham, the father of our faith, the apostles and prophets who founded the Church and even the Founding Fathers of America. It is no coincidence that foundation and fathers go together.

Dad, you have the awesome privilege and responsibility to lay the foundation for your children's lives. For all you moms who may be reading this and thinking, *What about my kids?* As I stated in the single moms chapter and generational momentum, if Dad is not there, then God will honor your faith too. Laying a foundation is crucial and it is hard work. No one sees the foundation or thinks about it when the house or building is complete. But make no mistake, the foundation is what holds the character of our children that we are building for God's purpose in this world.

Dad, it is hard work, but it is a work worth doing and certainly a work worth fighting for. So don't give up or compromise in this labor of love that you have in this mandate you have been given of pouring godly values and character into the young hearts God has trusted to you. You are to write on the tablet of their hearts that are a blank canvas. So use the pen of a ready writer and write God's Word on them. Model your faith for them to see, and impart God's wisdom into their lives. I know it is hard and you have a lot of important things to do and to take care of, but none are as important as this. In fact, you only get one shot to lay the foundation, one shot to raise your children up in the way they should go, so do it well and do it tirelessly with the love God the Father has given you.

This reminds me of the amazing story of a father by the name of Dick Hoyt.

The Hoyts

This dad literally knows that it is hard being the dad our children need. Eighty-five times he has pushed his disabled son, Rick, 26.2 miles in marathons. Eight times he has not only pushed him 26.2 miles in a wheel-chair, but also towed him 2.4 miles in a dinghy while swimming and pedaling him 112 miles in a seat on the handlebars — all in the same day.

Dick has pulled him cross-country skiing, taken him on his back mountain climbing and once hauled him across the U.S. on a bike. Rick was disabled from birth from the umbilical cord wrapped around his neck at birth. The doctors said, "He will be a vegetable the rest of his life."

When Rick was eleven, they took him to the Engineering Department at Tufts University and discovered that Rick could understand when he was spoken to. So they created a special computer that allowed him to control the cursor by touching a switch with the side of his head. Rick was finally able to communicate. Later, a high school classmate was paralyzed in an accident and the school organized a charity run for him. Rick expressed to his dad, "Dad, I want to do that." Dick, who never ran more than a mile at a time, was going to push his son five miles? Even so, he tried. That day changed Rick's life. "Dad," he typed, "when we were running, it felt like I wasn't disabled anymore!"

That day changed Dick's life. He became passionate with giving Rick that feeling as often as he could. In fact, he got into such great shape that he and Rick were ready to try the 1979 Boston marathon. Then in 1983, they ran another marathon so fast they made the qualifying time for Boston the following year. Then somebody suggested they try a triathlon, so here is a dad who never learned to swim and hadn't ridden a bike since he was six, signing up to haul his 110-pound son through a triathlon. You know what? He did and now they have done 212 triathlons, including four grueling 15-hour Ironman's in Hawaii. Why does this dad try so hard to do these things? Because he has discovered the power of touching his disabled son, no matter the cost or consequence. He had discovered what every dad does who pays the price. It is worth it. They are worth it. Dick does it purely for "the awesome feeling" he gets seeing his boy, Rick, smile as they run, swim and ride together with his hands lifted as they cross the finish line each time.

Rick believes in the power of touch his father has so selflessly offered him time and time again, and was quoted on his computer stating, "My dad is the father of the century."

Dick and Rick travel today speaking about their amazing journey and story of tragedy to triumph. The best part of the story is that Rick would like to give his dad a special gift and that is, "that my dad would sit in the chair and I would push him just once."

You owe it yourself to see this story on video. We have shown it in our church before, and there wasn't a dry eye in the house. Why? Because it's a story of God's grace and faithfulness. In fact, He is the Father who has always been pushing us. We are the ones who were crippled by sin, but His loving touch has pushed us through every limitation and hurt that kept us from winning too.

For millions in the last few decades, the father's touch has been missing for many in America, but God has good news for us. God is changing that! He is turning the hearts of fathers to the children, and when fathers turn to their children, the children turn back to their fathers.

My heart and sincere hope is to help encourage and equip every dad as well as granddads in touching their children and grandchildren. I want to help bring God's healing touch to every son and daughter who has been wounded, for those who have never felt the power of the Father's touch. If that's you today, I want you to know that God is here for you. All you have to do is reach out and ask Him to touch you in faith and He will. He has always wanted to, and He will never stop loving you.

BUILDING SELF-ESTEEM IN CHILDREN

Why is this important? Self-esteem is vital in a person's identity. Self-esteem is how we see ourselves. We reflect to others how we feel about ourselves. If I can't esteem myself, then I can't esteem others. If I don't feel good about who I am, then I will not feel good about others.

PEOPLE WITH LOW SELF-ESTEEM CAN BE...

- Performance based – being high achievers in an attempt to gain self-worth;

- Negative – they are critical of others because of the things they despise in themselves; and

- Ungrateful in attitude – bent towards compulsive complaining.

Here are some ways I have been taught that you can start using today to build healthy self-esteem in your children and grandchildren.

⇲ **Affection** – As I stated earlier, it has been clinically proven that children need affection, and it helps them develop into healthy, happy people. Dad, it's just not enough to be around, or to just say it. You have to show it. It doesn't matter if it is boys or girls. They need it. In fact, Dad, if your little girls don't get if from you, they will get it from somewhere and always for the wrong reason. Prostitutes have said they sold themselves to men initially to get the affection of a man they never received. Fatherlessness has driven many girls to the streets which has led many of these young girls into sexual exploitation. Affection says you are valuable. So kiss and hug your boys as long as they will let you. They need it too, and your girls even as they develop into young women. Even though her body is changing, she is still that little girl you held often when she was younger. She needs that healthy embrace of a Father to give her security. Look at the father of this twenty something year-old son in Luke 15:20:

*"So he returned home to his father. And while he was still a long way off, his father saw him coming. Filled with love and compassion, **he ran to his son, embraced him, and kissed him.**"*

I can confess to you that I kiss and hug my children every day of their lives that I see them. I do it in the morning when they leave for school, when they get home from school and at bedtime in the evening. I have fun with it by telling them I have to get as many as I can in case one day they don't let me anymore when they are grown. So dads and granddads, give them that affection they long for from you. They don't just need affection from mom when they are hurt or disappointed; they need it from us dads too. Give them affection, and if you are married, let them see you give it to their mother. Model it for them.

➢ **Affirmation** – This means we validate our children, claiming them as worthy and legitimate. If affection is physical touch, then this would be with words and with our body language. It has been said that 85 percent of what we say comes from our body language, meaning our faces and posture. Have you ever wondered what your face says, even when your mouth is closed? You should ask your children sometime.

I know all too well the ambition we can have to want to excel in our careers and ministries and that is important. However, we should make sure that we carve out the time regularly in our lives to slow down, hold our children while looking them in the eyes, telling them, "You are mine, and I am so pleased with you." God the Father modeled this for us.

Matthew 3:17 says, *"And a voice from heaven said, 'This is my dearly loved Son, who brings me great joy.'"* We have power in our words. In fact, the power of life and death are in the tongue (Proverbs 18:21). Did you download that, Dad? Life and death are in our tongues, so let's decide to use it to bring life into our children daily.

Honestly, dads, we can sometimes be overly harsh and critical, but let's commit today to use our words to build up our children and bless them. Let's be slow to criticize and quick to praise. They say it takes eight positives to negate one negative.

I heard about a man who played for the Houston Oilers who had never had the pleasure of his father coming to watch his game ever. Having made it to the NFL, he had seats reserved at every home game for his father, and one day his dad came to see him play. He played like an all-pro. He had five tackles, a sack and blocked a field goal. At the end of the game, he went straight to his dad to hear affirmation, but his father's only words were, "If you had been a little faster, you could have done more."

He stated that something in him died that day, and he lost the desire to ever play sports anymore. He eventually quit the NFL and turned to a life of drugs and alcohol. His father's words crushed him on the inside that day. That's why I am encouraging you, dads, to understand and remember the power of your words.

Let me be the first to say that I am not perfect and I have said some things that I have had to repent of. I had to tell my children, "I am sorry. That was wrong for me to say that. Please forgive me." If you have missed it, you need to know that it's good for our children to see us live out our faith. If we miss it, then we should make it right. In fact, I think it reinforces our faith in the hearts of our children. Dads, it is so important for us as fathers to validate our children and to encourage them in their dreams.

THE HEART OF A SON IS SHAPED IN THE BREATH OF A FATHER

I love the story of one dad named Zechariah from Luke, chapter 1, who was filled with the Holy Spirit and also spoke prophetically over his son, John, about his destiny. I see this as the highest form of fathering, because as his dad, he was the spiritual leader of the family. He was obedient to God and filled with the Holy Spirit. He called him what God called him, not what He wanted to call him. Dad, may this teach us that it is not our job to tell them *WHAT* they are to become, but to tell them *WHO* they are, that they are sons and daughters first. We are not to try to make them into our image, but into God's image, to see their gifts and passions and speak to them, confirm and call them out. We are not to tell them what they should be or do because we think that is what they should be and do. But we need to know what God wants them to be and do. That can only come as we spend time with Him and get full of His Spirit.

I tell my children Michael, Presley, and Madelyn, "I see this gift in you or this potential to do this in you. Rise up and give it your all. Do your best, be your best and look your best. God is going to use you in a mighty way in this area. I acknowledge this, so do it. God put it in you, and I believe in you!"

I think it's interesting that God had to seal Zechariah's mouth or he may have called John something else that he wanted. When he submitted to God's will, God loosed his tongue and gave him a powerful word for his son as recorded in Luke 1:67-80:

Then his father, Zechariah, was filled with the Holy Spirit and gave this prophecy:

"Praise the Lord, the God of Israel,

>*because he has visited and redeemed his people.*

He has sent us a mighty Savior

>*from the royal line of his servant David,*

just as he promised

>*through his holy prophets long ago.*

Now we will be saved from our enemies

>*and from all who hate us.*

He has been merciful to our ancestors

>*by remembering his sacred covenant —*

the covenant he swore with an oath

>*to our ancestor Abraham.*

We have been rescued from our enemies

>*so we can serve God without fear,*

in holiness and righteousness

>*for as long as we live.*

And you, my little son,

>*will be called the prophet of the Most High,*

>*because you will prepare the way for the Lord.*

You will tell his people how to find salvation

>*through forgiveness of their sins.*

Because of God's tender mercy,

the morning light from heaven is about to break upon us,

to give light to those who sit in darkness and in the shadow of death,

and to guide us to the path of peace."

John grew up and became strong in spirit. And he lived in the wilderness until he began his public ministry to Israel.

Zechariah prayed and declared John's destiny as he was plugged in to the Holy Spirit. We, as fathers who are Christ followers, should seek the Lord, be filled with His Spirit and make prophetic declarations from what we sense God is putting into our hearts about our children's future in the Lord. We, like Zechariah, can be used of God to make a straight path for them to walk forth on. We can declare a spiritual foundation to launch them into their destiny.

Psalm 127 says that our children are like arrows in the hands of a warrior. We are to shape those arrowheads, because if we don't, they won't hit the target.

We are the ones who shape them and pull back the bow to shoot them towards God's amazing purpose for their lives that will bring honor to Him in their lifetime! We have the awesome privilege of being used by our heavenly Father to shape them, mold them and aim them towards their purpose. We are to eventually release them and know that we helped aim them into adulthood so they can go further and faster than we did to fulfill God's perfect will for their lives in their generation!

Dad, if we don't, then they will not hit their target. They will miss their mark, which in essence is the definition of sin: missing the mark. We don't want that, but remember, we are called by God as warriors to fight the good fight of faith. We are to fight for our integrity and for our Christ-centered values by not compromising with what the world says is acceptable! We are to fight for our homes, marriages and for our children.

Arrowheads are shaped to hit the target and as dads we are to shape them with care, love and discipline approved of by God. If we don't, they may not hit the mark. In fact, the results of our culture show that they are twenty times more likely to end up in prison. Once we let them go, we can't grab them while in route to their target, meaning that if we shape them correctly, we can rest assured that once they come to the age of accountability where they have to make their own choices, they will still hit the target. It is vital to know that you are not just raising your children, but you are raising your grandchildren's parents.

Maybe your child is older now and you didn't get to start off right. It is never too late and God's Word can change any situation. Even if your child is older, in teen years or older, and they seem unstable, you can speak the promises of God's Word over them as well as to them in the name of Jesus.

We saw that Jesus validated Peter and helped him to see who he was. As Jesus said, "No longer will you be called Simon," which means shaky reed, "but Peter," which means rock. He spoke into Peter's life as a father would a son. That helped to bring stability to Peter's unstable nature. God can change your child's heart through the power of His Spirit and through your words to him or her.

The next thing we can give our children to build self-esteem is....

➢ **Acceptance** – our acceptance of who God wants them to be produces security. Accepting them for who they are even if they aren't just like you. Billy Joel sang it best – I love you just the way you are. Love them where they are and lead them where they need to go. Give them your love and they will follow your lead. I have learned that they will buy into my message after they have bought into the man. Even if you love sports and they don't. Even if they love math and not ministry. Even if they love to create art and not hunt or fish. If you will accept them and learn to love what they love, they will let you into their world. I am not talking about accepting lifestyle choices, relationships or habits that contradict God's Word, but rather particular preferences of passions.

They want to know what we think and what we think is very heavy in their minds. We must handle this great power with great care and precision. What we say and think as Dad carries a lot of weight. Again, remember Dads, our words have the power to develop or destroy our children's worldview as well as the view of themselves. Let's follow God the Father when it comes to acceptance knowing that we have been accepted by God's love for us as sons and daughters, not for who we should be or could be, but just as we are.

Lastly, building self-esteem is celebrating their…

➢ **Achievement** – As dads, let's acknowledge all their accomplishments. That means we put up their artwork around the house and office, report cards, trophies, even for the little ones. That means we make it to the plays, shows, games, recitals and graduations. We make it to the birthday parties and donuts for dads. We celebrate their education and report cards. Dads, we need to help with homework when we can and go to eat lunch with them at school as long as they will let us. Be active in their lives and in the things they enjoy. Get into their world and make a difference. That continues into their teen years, college and beyond. Even as fathers of grown children, we should point out and celebrate all they do.

I have been to mental math, spelling bees, choruses, plays, dance recitals and games to watch cheerleading. In fact, during football we attend three different games every Saturday for all three children. Dads, our children need us to support their achievements. The games I played the hardest were the ones my dad attended. Still today it gives me a thrill to share with my dad about anything I am doing personally or as a father. I love it when my spiritual father and stepdad are proud of me and my achievements in life that I am currently doing. As I stated in an earlier chapter, it is a huge motivating factor.

I coach my two boys in the sports they play. I have coached their baseball, basketball and football teams just to be around them. I remember how special that was for me as a boy the two seasons that I was able to experience with my father. I recall my oldest boy Michael has always wanted to score a touchdown, but has only been asked to run the ball three or four times by the offensive coach. He started as a defensive tackle and in his fourth year, he was blessed with the opportunity to pick up a blocked punt and run into the end zone for his first touchdown ever. I can't tell you how I soared with excitement for him, but what really reminded me that sons want acknowledgement of their accomplishments was the fact that as he went into the end zone and his teammates were patting him on the helmet, he held up the ball in the air looking to the sidelines to show me what he had done. I will tell you how it just melted my heart. He wanted his dad to watch him succeed and celebrate with him. He was looking for Dad's affirmation of what he had accomplished.

Then there was the time my other son hit a grand slam homerun to end the game. I was there in the dugout, and he ran straight to me for fist bumps. I can't forget the dance recital Madelyn was in, I am not into ballet, but when she was on the stage, I was all into ballet because she was there.

Find ways to celebrate all of your children's achievements even if they are small. If they get a job or a promotion, even if you think it's menial, celebrate it and tell them, "Good job," That will cause them to want to be their very best for Dad. It lets them know that you are watching and that you are proud of them.

Laying on of Hands

As we wrap us this chapter, I want to leave you with a charge to touch your children often in all the ways we discussed in this chapter. I want you to lay your hands on your children and speak over their lives, regardless of their age. You see, it represents blessing and transfer of authority. We need to crown our children to become the kings and queens God has called them to be so they can rule in life, take dominion, be conquering overcomers, not victims of defeat and insecurity who have little or no self-esteem. Dads, we love you and we need you, so build us up like only you can!

Dad, maybe you have read this and realize that you have never had the affection or acceptance of a father. I have been there, and I want you to know, God is here and He desperately wants you to know how much He cares. May you hear His voice and embrace today, saying, "I love you. I believe in you. I celebrate you," God wants you to know He is pulling for you and He has plans to do you good, plans to give you hope and a future. It is never too late to start being a great father. This is why we have to be healed at the cross and understand that we have been adopted by God as sons and daughters in order to be the fathers and mothers He purposes us to be. Why not accept His love today?

CHAPTER 10

Single Moms, "Rise Up!"

ONE RECENT STUDY I read from the U.S. Census Bureau said that 38 percent of mothers in our country today are single. Many of them live below the poverty level. Some are single due to the incarceration of the children's father. Most of them are left to fill the void of the fathers in the lives of their children.

When fathers are not in their God-designed place in the family, the mother rises up to fulfill the role of Dad. Now, please understand that I am not knocking any single dads out there, because the number of single dads are on the rise as well. I personally know many single dads who are great dads and are heavily involved in their children's lives. I applaud those who are as that can be a challenging dynamic, to say the least when it comes to fathering your children effectively and you only see them every other weekend. I will touch on that in another chapter.

For most single moms that I know, including my own, they do not have the benefit of a dad who is taking action to be involved in raising and fathering his children. As my good friend, Dale Bronner says, "The problem with fatherlessness is usually the childishness of men."

I want to take just a moment here to encourage all of the mamas out there who are working, paying the bills, cutting the grass, helping with homework, being team mom, driving the kids to every event and praying your guts out trying to keep your nose above water, you are heroines in our culture. If it weren't for you stepping up to fill the shoes of a mother and a father, the lives of those of us without the benefit of a two-parent household, would have not had a chance in life at all. Thank you!

My mother raised me, mostly since I was seven years old. I can tell you that she worked hard to do all those things. She was providing and allowing me to be involved with sports. I know she sacrificed a lot to give me a better life than the one she experienced. Looking back, I am amazed at the amount of patience, faithfulness and love she gave out when not a lot of it came back.

For those of you who are single moms reading this book, you know better than anyone what I am talking about. Your dedication and strength amaze me as you have had to walk through parenthood perhaps alone at times with no one to encourage you or to lean on in all those moments of shear pandemonium. I hope this chapter inspires you to keep on keeping on so that you will see this verse from Proverbs actually take place in your latter years. *"Her children rise up and call her blessed ..."* (Proverbs 31:28 NKJV). You can do it. You can make it. Don't quit, no matter what!

SON OF MY SORROW

In the book of Genesis, there was a mother named Rachel who was giving birth to a son who literally caused her to die. In the last moments of her life, with the birth of her newborn, she called the baby Ben-Oni, which means "son of my sorrow." The baby's father, Jacob, however, decided the name of this child and called him Benjamin, which means "son of my right hand" (See Genesis 35:18). Jacob renamed him Benjamin ("son of my right hand"). Jacob turned this occasion of sorrow into triumph and a victorious prospect. In addition, he wanted to give a good name to the child who was the answer to Rachel's prayer (Genesis 30:23).

Your child is a son or daughter of God's right hand, literally meaning that they are particularly dear and precious. He is a father to the fatherless. Maybe you are a single mom. You may feel like your son or daughter has caused you sorrow and it is about to kill you. But know that if you are in covenant with God the Father, He has called them and He will save them and transform them so they will have a name change. They will be a son of His right hand, in Christ, who is seated at the right hand of the Father in heaven!

The father called him "the son of my right hand." You may feel like you have failed as a mother and that maybe God made a mistake. You may believe it has been all wrong with your child, but you must believe that God is going to make it all right. The right hand symbolizes authority, and that is where Jesus is seated. Because of what He accomplished through His death and resurrection, He holds the authority to reach your son or daughter. No matter how far away or how wrong they may be living right now, I know firsthand how true that is. As I wrote earlier, I was that son who brought my mother much sorrow and pain. I was raised by my mom for the majority of my childhood.

When I was nine, my single mother did the single greatest act anyone could do. She took me to a life-giving church where I felt God's presence and love for the first time ever. It was there that I gave my heart to Jesus Christ! We joined the church and we were there literally every time the doors were open; Sunday mornings and evenings, every Wednesday as well, not to mention the week-long revivals. I did not mind because I loved being in the company of this church family, singing with such passion and joy to this great God we loved so much.

It wasn't that bad until I hit my teen years. As with many teens, even if both parents are involved, it can be challenging to a parent, but I think perhaps especially in the case of a single mom, and even more so with a son. I began to push back against my mother's authority, and all authority for that matter. I had this brewing anger in me and didn't know why until after I was actually a man. I understood the scripture in Ephesians 6:4: *"Fathers, do not provoke your children to anger by the way you treat them. Rather, bring them up with the discipline and instruction that comes from the Lord."*

When fathers don't love their children enough or don't know how to bring them up in the discipline and instruction of the Lord, it provokes them to anger. I will speak more on this in another chapter.

I would not apply myself in school or study for any class. I found myself in the principal's office more often than ever. I was on my way to full-blown rebellion. Entering my freshman year of high school, I had drifted from my genuine faith and love for God's house. I fought my mother tooth and nail about going to church. Unfortunately, I finally won that battle and she would go without me at least for a season.

Now her son, who had once brought her joy, was bringing a lot of sorrow to her life. It was about to get worse. As I continued to get involved with the wrong crowd, there was more exposure to smoking, drugs and alcohol as well as sexual promiscuity. As my grades continued to go south, so did my attitude and my desire to play sports or excel at anything.

Now with multiple suspensions from school for fighting, skipping school or just flat out verbal confrontation with teachers, my mom had nothing to be proud of in our community when it came to her only son. This should have been the best years of a parent's life, to see their child shine and make them glad they had children. The joy of seeing your child excel and reach their potential is the goal of every sensible parent. This was not the case for my mother as I eventually rolled the dice too often and lost. I came up short my senior year and could not graduate. The embarrassment of having to explain to family and friends why your child didn't graduate only added to the sorrow that piled up in her life.

I chose to not complete the course the next year and put off the completion of my GED to a future date. Having left high school, I now set my sights on getting a job and getting out of my mother's house. It didn't take long to figure out that education would have really helped as I filled out multiple applications for employment. I became increasingly aware that I was leaving my father's house to go out into the world to do my own thing. I soon found out that I would not be able to do anything that would challenge me or cause me to want to give my everything for. I worked sporadically, bouncing from job to job with no vision, no purpose. The only vision I had was Friday and getting out of whatever job I could hold down for any length of time with very little pay. It led me to more substance and alcohol abuse to where eventually I was caught by an undercover officer in the parking lot of a nightclub at nineteen years of age.

The sorrow my mother must have felt watching her only son walk out of the Fulton County Jail that night must have been almost too much to bear. I know firsthand how one's life as a son or daughter can bring much sorrow to a single mom who feels like dying at times.

Maybe you are reading this thinking, *Michael, you are speaking to me.* I do have good news for you. There is hope. There is a God, a Father, who hears you and cares for your child even more than you do. He is well able to watch after your children and save them. He can turn their life around and alleviate the source of your sorrow; God can cause you to feel joy in the future.

As you may already know, God does have plans for them, and if anyone can turn this thing around, it is God! His arm is not too short to reach them, wherever they may be. They can't escape His love for them.

What's a Mother to Do?

Let me offer some practical steps that you can apply now in your child's life. I want to introduce you to another great single mom, Eunice, who was actually impacted by her mother, Lois. We see the Apostle Paul referring to their faith when addressing his apprentice pastor, Tim, in 2 Timothy 1:5, *"I remember your genuine faith, for you share the faith that first filled your grandmother Lois and your mother, Eunice. And I know that same faith continues strong in you."* The faith Timothy was growing in was nurtured by his grandmother and mother, who was single as Timothy's father was Greek and was said to have died at an early age. What did they do to pass that along? What does the Bible teach us on this?

While in prison, Paul wrote Timothy a couple of letters to instruct and encourage Timothy as a pastor. We know those letters as 1 and 2 Timothy. Let's look at 2 Timothy to show how a mom can leave a godly legacy to her children, even if she finds herself doing it without the help of a man.

Inspire a love for God's Word. A mom can raise godly children by inspiring a love for Scripture in her kids, which is the model we see laid out by these two great mothers of faith!

Second Timothy 3:15 says, *"You have been taught the holy Scriptures from childhood, and they have given you the wisdom to receive the salvation that comes by trusting in Christ Jesus."*

So from childhood, you are encouraged to teach your children the Word of God, especially if your children are younger. This principle is huge. But don't worry! Even if they are older now, the Word still works in the heart of every child, regardless of their age.

When Timothy was just a baby, perhaps before he could crawl or feed himself, Eunice began teaching him Scripture. As Timothy grew up, he was taught Bible stories about David and Goliath, Samson and Delilah, Elijah and the prophets of Baal. The Word of God shaped young Timothy's mind, heart and imagination.

This is what my mom did for me when I was running in the opposite direction of God. That is, praying effectively. It's true, prayer does change things. This is never truer than when a loving mother goes before the Lord in prayer on behalf of her child. I am living proof of the power of a praying mama. My mother told me that every time I walked out the door, she would pray and declare the blood of Jesus over my life. Eternity will only tell just how important that was and how it saved me from dying in my wild, foolish living.

It reminds me of the story of a mother in the Bible whose daughter was possessed by a demon. She took it to Jesus. She asked for His help. Jesus ignored her and then denied her, but she wasn't having it. She came and knelt before Him, and said, "Lord, help me." She kept asking, seeking and knocking. Finally, after humbling herself and having a tenacious prayer of faith, she interceded for her daughter and Jesus sent His Word and healed her daughter.

She interceded? What does that mean at a grassroots level? It basically means to intersect God's will with someone else's. In other words, she took hold of Jesus and then took hold of her daughter, spiritually speaking. She asked for God to cause her to encounter the power of Jesus Christ. Her daughter couldn't ask for herself as she was possessed by a demon. She interceded by bringing her daughter to God's will for her life, which was to be set free and healed (See Luke 4:18), and that's what happened.

Mom, you may feel helpless in influencing your child right now. Maybe they are very far from God right now and living a life that is being influenced by the demonic powers of hell. They are blinded by Satan and can't see the glory of Christ (2 Corinthians 4:4). You may feel like all you can do is pray. Can I remind you that you have been given this powerful arsenal called prayer at your disposal? If you have turned to Christ and are filled with the Holy Spirit, then God gives us this promise in John 14:13: *"You can ask for anything in my name, and I will do it, so that the Son can bring glory to the Father."*

He said you can ask anything that would cause the Son to bring glory to the Father. What a divine opportunity for you to pray prayers of faith, knowing that seeing your child set free and serving God in his or her generation is definitely something that would cause glory to be given to the Father through the Son, Jesus.

Mom, right now you can come before the Almighty God of heaven and earth in faith. You can thank God for who He is and acknowledge that He is holy and that He is Lord. Grab hold of God in one hand, and then you can call out your child's name to Him. Begin to ask that God would open their eyes, that God would cause them to encounter the power of Jesus Christ, that Jesus would heal them and set them free. Pray to the Lord of the harvest to send laborers into their lives, just like He told us to in Matthew 9:38: *"So pray to the Lord who is in charge of the harvest; ask him to send more workers into his fields."* Pray that God would send people into their lives to be a witness to them and shine God's love into their world.

You can pray until you have caused them to intersect with God's will. You can pray that your child would know God as Father and Lord. You can pray that your child would serve God in their generation and fulfill their purpose. When you do, just know that it is only a matter of time. Rise up and believe that help is on the way! I tell students and anybody really, if you have a praying mama, just go ahead and surrender, because you are heading towards a direct encounter with Jesus Christ!

What You Do Speaks Much Louder Than What You Say

Lastly, you should model your genuine, authentic faith. To help raise godly children, you should give them a godly example to follow.

Second Timothy 1:5 NIV says, *"I have been reminded of your sincere faith, which first lived in your grandmother Lois and in your mother Eunice and, I am persuaded, now lives in you also."* "Sincere" literally means "without hypocrisy." Timothy's faith was real, genuine, authentic. It wasn't fake. It was not for show. Timothy was the real deal. He was totally sold out to Jesus, fully devoted, completely surrendered to God.

Where did Timothy see such an authentic faith? He learned it from his mom and grandmother. Timothy grew up in a home with two women who had a genuine faith in God. They not only talked the talk, they walked the walk. When moms model an authentic faith, they create an environment for their children to develop an authentic faith too. It's worth noting that nothing is said here about a father. Not even Paul gave himself credit for the strength and validity of Timothy's faith. Moms, it is possible for you to raise godly children, even without the help of a father or grandfather, not insinuating that we don't need fathers, because as I said before, we all have that internal need for a father. But my point is that if you have found yourself in a situation without a man or a father who can pass on his faith, you still can. But you need to live out your authentic faith yourself if you want to pass it on to your children.

Mom, to raise up a Timothy, "one who honors God," you have to take your faith seriously. You can't just go through the motions spiritually. You can't delegate that calling to the church's children's pastor, youth pastor or senior pastor. You can't delegate that to the best Christian school in the world. These can add to what you are doing and partner with you in that development, but your faith needs to be real, genuine and authentic. Your children need to see you consistently reading the Bible. I would say, even let them catch you reading the Bible, praying, worshiping, serving and living for the glory of God. Determine that it will be at the top of your list in raising up children who will honor God, if not today, then one day.

I heard of a statistic once that said if a child attends church and their parents/parent doesn't live out what they say they believe, if they attend church every Sunday, but don't model their faith and live out biblical values, that when that child turns eighteen, 92 percent leave the church, never to return. They don't see the point of using their Sundays to attend a church when there are plenty of other things to do with their time. In their eyes, it was simply a social choice, not a conviction. So when they have the choice to choose, they choose something else.

However, the same study revealed that when parents/a parent who attended church regularly and did model their faith that only 10 percent of children when they turned eighteen left church on a regular basis, and of those, many returned when they had families on their own, which reminds me of something Proverbs teaches. Proverbs 22:6 NKJV says, *"Train up a child in the way he should go, and when he is old he will not depart from it."*

Moms, raising children who will honor God is hard work, but it is good work, a worthwhile, important work. And for those moms who are raising children without much if any help from a man, you need to know your assignment isn't easy, but it is not impossible either. You can do it. You can make it. Don't quit, no matter what!

I read a story about four scholars who were arguing over Bible translations. One said he preferred the *King James Version* because of its beauty and eloquence. Another said he liked the *New American Standard Version* for its literalism and accuracy. The third scholar loved the *New Living Translation* for its use of contemporary phrases and idioms. After being quiet for a moment, the fourth scholar admitted, "I personally prefer my mother's translation." When the other scholars started laughing, he said, "Yes, she has translated the Scriptures. My mom has translated each page of the Bible into life. And it's the most convincing translation I have ever read."

One Who Honors God

So Mom, it is paramount that you find a life-giving church, join there and get planted. Find one that really focuses on raising up the next generation. Plug into the vision, start giving, serving and join a small group. Show your children your faith; don't just tell them what it is. They are watching you, and I truly believe that the greatest gift we can transfer to the next generation is our values rooted in God's Word and God's house. I am so grateful now to my mother for following the leading of the Lord, digging in to a powerful life-giving church. Thinking back I reflect on some of the ways my mom modeled her faith. I remember my mom praying, reading her Bible and listening to gospel music every morning before school as she would prepare for work. So I basically woke up every morning to a house filled with praise and worship, probably one big reason I love it so much and actually wake my own children up with it now.

I can remember her serving in Sunday school, and every time the offering came around she would put what seemed to be large amounts of cash in the offering. I now know that she committed $125.00 a month to our church's building program. She later told me that she would work overtime at work just to be able to give what she committed to for God's Kingdom.

My memories of her serving, attending and giving financially above and beyond her means, were making impressions in my young Christian heart that would not show up until many, many years later. As one who walked this path of growing up in the home of a single mother, knowing what I know now, in hindsight, some of these examples may seem small and insignificant, but make no mistake, these seeds may have been as small as mustard seeds, but the power of God lies inside even the tiniest of seeds.

Then He said, "What is the kingdom of God like? And to what shall I compare it? It is like a mustard seed, which a man took and put in his garden: and it grew and became a large tree, and the birds of the air nested in its branches" (Luke 13:18,19 NKJV).

You see, these small seeds that you sow into your child's life may have small beginnings. In fact, it may seem as if nothing is happening. However, in the soil of their hearts, those seeds are taking root and will one day sprout into a life of blessing that has the power to bless many lives, including your own!

In my own life, even through all the junk and all the bad seeds the enemy sowed in my life, God has caused these small seeds to grow twenty years later into a phenomenal harvest of blessing in my life as well as in the lives of those I have the honor of leading. What I am trying to say to you is, don't be discouraged, don't quit as Paul says in Galatians 6:9 NKJV: *"And let us not grow weary while doing good, for in due season we shall reap if we do not lose heart."*

Mom, remember that as you serve God by developing your relationship with Him and model your faith in front of your children, you are setting them up for later in life when they will reflect the model they have seen in you. Don't give up, because there is a due season of blessing waiting for you in your future!

WHAT ABOUT THEIR FATHER?

Let me speak to you concerning this delicate area of your heart towards your children's father. First off, since we are talking about seeds, let's look at Galatians 6:7: *"Don't be misled — you cannot mock the justice of God. You will always harvest what you plant."* Honor is a seed and it has a sound. We are to honor all people, and I will speak more on this later. What I want to point out here is that the way of honor is not always easy, but it is always best. Honor is God's way and it does bring a reward with it. Knowing firsthand about the sensitivity to this subject when it comes to the area of you as a single mom daring to conceive the idea of honoring the man who perhaps dishonored you, leaving you and the children high and dry may be a stretch, but go with me for a minute. To honor him is to honor God.

It is a real temptation to inform your children of just how bad their father is so they won't be deceived as you were and to lead them into more pain. I get it, I understand, but you must embrace God's way so that you do not transfer your hurt, anger and iniquity to the next generation.

"Iniquity" means to be bent towards something, Let Jesus straighten it out through your actions of faith. You don't want to pass that down to your children as God has commanded to honor our fathers regardless of if they are worthy of it or not.

I know because I remember the tears of my mother and the anger she had towards my father. I remember the betrayals of trust more than once and how intense the pain can be for a single mother, not firsthand of course, but from a child's perspective. No child wants to see their mother cry. You may even feel that it's okay to ask your child about their father or be tempted to send messages through your child, but please don't let them get caught in the cross fire. They are innocent in the matter, so protect them from drive-by guilt and tongue assaults aimed at their father or some other woman involved. It seems natural to project the father in a negative way, but it will make it harder for your child to fulfill God's will in forgiveness and honor later in life.

I am not advocating misrepresenting the failures or shortcomings of what the man did or is doing, but the tone in which you do it is key. You see, honor has a sound. When I am considering someone in our church for leadership, I always listen to what they say and how they speak about people, because honor has a tone to it. As wrong as he may have been, God is still able to right that wrong. You can actually be a part of the healing process for yourself, your children and their father. It is always important to remember that while we were still sinners, Christ shed His blood for us. Christ shed His blood for you, your children and their father. God loves you all. It may seem as if their father is the enemy, but again, remember that we have only one enemy and that is Satan. He is the adversary who has done this. He is the one who came to steal, kill and destroy.

Your Story Can End Well

She may have never seen it coming, but God did. Let me share a moment of how God didn't forget about all those tears or those seeds my mom had sown many years ago. When I was twenty-four, I nearly encountered death in a hospital after having been out indulging in drugs and alcohol. Shortly thereafter, I began to desire to get right with God, to go back to church and try to make peace with Him. I took baby steps and was struggling until I had an encounter with the Lord that totally set me free and changed my life. I was free and I was going after God full throttle.

I knew I had to get out of the county I had grown up in. I asked if I could move in with my mother who lived on the other side of metro Atlanta, along with her new husband. My mother wasn't serving the Lord at the time nor was my stepdad. I landed a pretty good job and began Bible College later that same year. God was using my life to influence my mother who fifteen years earlier had influenced mine. He was not only influencing hers, but my stepdad's as well.

It wasn't long thereafter that they began attending church with me every Sunday. They began to get involved and joined the church. It was a beautiful thing. A couple of years later, the Lord gave them an idea for a business, so they stepped out to do it. They expected to do about a half a million in business that first year and doubled that. God continued to prosper and empower them to give to the church to help pay off the debt of the church building. He eventually would use their business to help fund the church plant we launched nine years ago.

In my mind, I went back to all those times the offering plate was passing us back in the mid eighties sowing into that building. Seeds, seeds, seeds, all those seeds coming back that she had sowed so faithfully when I was a boy.

Can you believe it? God took this messed-up Georgia boy who came from a broken home, raised by this little five foot tall single mom and eventually used them to plant a life-giving church that has impacted thousands of lives for the glory of God? You see, Mom, no matter how bad it is today, if you will only believe, trust God, continue to live out your faith and don't stop sowing those seeds, you will see the glory of God in your life and in the lives of your children's children.

Maybe you are in the sowing season of your life. Continue to serve, sow and believe that those seeds will come back to you. It may be one year, ten years or twenty years, but be assured that they will come back to you to bless you and that your latter years will be your best because of God's never-ending love for you and your children. Who knows if you are raising up a future pastor, church planter, father, mother, artist, author, leader, worship leader, Christian business person, doctor or inventor who will change the world as we know it. What do single moms do? They rise up!

CHAPTER 11

Not Many Fathers

FIRST CORINTHIANS 4:15 NKJV states, *"For though you might have ten thousand instructors in Christ, yet you do not have many fathers...."*

Paul was writing to the church that was birthed from his spiritual journey as he preached the gospel of Jesus Christ. People would be saved and then the plan was that they grow in their faith, gifting and calling. He reminds them that he was a spiritual father to them, that he was more than a guardian and he loved them like a father does his children... or should love them, I might add. It is true spiritually, but isn't it true naturally too?

In chapter 2, we examined the evidence and it is clear that we don't have many fathers spiritually or naturally. For this reason, I want to speak in this chapter to those of us who don't have a father, spiritually or naturally. I want to speak to all who are fathers as well and what you can do to allow God to heal our land. God wants to use you to raise up the next generation naturally and spiritually! God has called us to make a difference in the lives of others. This is especially true for us who are fathers or potential fathers.

The Need for Spiritual Fathers

There is an interesting story in the Gospel of Matthew, chapter 21, about Jesus' triumphant entry to the city of Jerusalem. Jesus needs a ride, so he sends a couple of His apostles to get a donkey's colt that is tied up at the moment, and oh, yes, did I mention that it belonged to someone else? So Jesus tells them where to find the colt and if asked by its owner, tell him the Lord has need of it.

The disciples go out to where the Lord told them to go, and sure enough, there was the colt and its <u>mother</u> when the disciples came for him. The disciples took him, laid their clothes on him and brought him to Jesus so that He could fulfill this prophetic word concerning Him about how their King would come riding on a donkey's colt.

Matthew 21:5 NIV says, *"Say to the Daughter of Zion, 'See, your king comes to you, gentle and riding on a donkey, on a colt, the foal of a donkey.'"* This was originally given through Zechariah (See Zechariah 9:9).

The apostles go to the place Jesus said to go and found the donkeys just like He said. They did something that may be common, but I think it could speak prophetically to something else as well. Just walk this way with me for a minute, and let's consider what else we could read into this story.

The donkey was a colt (a son?). The mother was there but no father? To me, I see this young, never-ridden colt, without the presence of a father in His life, that the Lord was calling and saying, "I have need of him. I am going to use this fatherless colt to do something he has never done before. I am going to ride him into destiny. I am going to let him carry Me to a city to change the world."

The apostles laid their cloaks on him and on his mother, which could speak of a modern-day application where God is restoring terms like "apostolic covering." This term may mean many things to many people, and wherever you stand on this nonessential is up to you. As far as I am concerned and the point I am making here is that I see myself and really all who have been in a fatherless situation in their lives. By that, I mean I see this young male tied up and bound with his mother, no father is around, and the Lord sends two apostles (spiritual fathers) to go untie them, set them free, cover them and take them to Jesus for their God-given purpose.

God is restoring spiritual fathers to the Body of Christ to help bring healing to the fatherless generations of our land. I believe that as they go, they will reach out to these lost sons and daughters who may be bound up in sin, hurt or addiction. They are fatherless, and God is sending them out through the local church. They will cover them with the Father's love. It is the touch of a godly father that will bring stability to their lives, and they will help usher in the return of the Lord Jesus Christ, just as this young colt ushered Jesus into Jerusalem in what is known as the triumphant entry. So too will these restored sons and daughters be used by God to usher in the imminent, triumphant return of Jesus Christ! The first time He rode on a donkey as a suffering servant, the next time He will be riding on a white horse as a conquering King!

The apostles are considered the fathers of the Church. Still today, one of the main characteristics of one of the gifts to the Body of Christ is an apostle (Ephesians 4:11). Again, I wish to reiterate the fact that maybe you don't believe they exist today, but that's not my point. My point is simply, God is restoring spiritual fathers back to the Body of Christ. Yes, some may pollute these terms and functions with selfish ambition or ulterior motives as I have personally seen in others. But what I will confirm is that there are true, genuine, authentic, God-loving fathers in the Body of Christ who are bringing healing to many.

Paul was definitely an apostle who had the nature and calling of a spiritual father. A spiritual father offers love, security and validation to sons and daughters of God who are connected in covenant. Spiritual fathers also validate sons and daughters to empower them for their life purpose. They help them with their identity by assisting them in establishing who they are in Jesus Christ.

I can only relate this to my personal journey and other pastor friends I have met during the last fifteen years. I personally believe that every person needs a father and every person needs to be validated. God knew that is exactly what I needed. I say this as one not having had an active father in my life, and then having spiritual fathers in my life who nurtured me, coached me and corrected me in love. It was a spiritual father who embraced me, laid his hands on me to bless me and crowned me as a man so I could flourish in manhood, marriage and ministry. I can say with certainty that it was a proven spiritual father who helped to establish me and helped me pass from being a boy to a man.

Still today, I meet annually with a spiritual father on a two-day retreat, along with other pastors who are spiritual sons, to receive impartation, wisdom and strength from a father. A mentor teaches you what he knows, but a father imparts who he is. I can't tell you the value of knowing that you have a spiritual father praying for you and supporting you in your purpose. It has been such a comfort and support, knowing that I am always within a phone call away from my spiritual fathers. It has allowed God to free me from fear of failure, fear of loneliness and has also fostered confidence in me as a son!

It was so important for me to learn how to live as a son so that I could become a good father. When we are raising our kids, it is vital to teach them to know what it means to be a son or a daughter so they can be good fathers and mothers. We are raising our grandchildren's parents. That's huge! I also believe spiritually that we need to learn what it means to be sons and daughters so we can be good spiritual leaders, fathers, mothers and mentors.

This generation coming up feels abandoned and orphaned. They are crying out for someone to recognize them, love them and to believe in them. God had to teach me how to live like a son so I could be a father to my children and a spiritual father to others. I am so humbled to think that others consider me a spiritual father, and I want to be sure to do my best in being that for them.

It is here that I want to mention some benefits of having a spiritual father, leader or pastor who can represent the Father to you. There are different levels in this area as Jesus had the seventy disciples, then the twelve, the three, and then John who was somehow closest to Jesus, that Jesus entrusted His mother Mary to his care.

What Do They Do?

The Apostle Paul was a godly father of the faith (1 Timothy1:2-16). Timothy was his spiritual son. Here was a young man who says his dad was Greek, but he is never mentioned again. Scripture says he had the faith of his mother and grandmother, but no mention of a father. Paul saw potential in this young man and began to mentor him and father him to validate him as a son. The name "Timothy" means "one who honors God."

Paul referred to Timothy as "my true son" (v. 2). God uses spiritual fathers to help those who feel abandoned or invalidated. They make them feel like a true child, a genuine child, an authentic heir. Paul made Timothy feel like he was validated and accepted as a son. It helps us know our place in the house of God and makes us feel secure in our identity. When you know this, you don't feel uncomfortable in your own skin or in church. That's exactly what spiritual fathers do for us, and it is what they should do for those they lead and love.

For those who may not have had a father, spiritually or naturally, I know God wants to raise you up as a son or daughter, as a Timothy, "one who honors God," in His house.

This is ultimately how God wants to use spiritual fathers in our lives. Spiritual fathers also cover us. I mean, they cover us in prayer. They teach us the Word of God. They cover us from folly and foolishness. They cover us with wise counsel when we need it. Spiritual fathers also comfort us. They comfort us when we pour out our hearts to them, and at times when we need to vent. They remind us of God's faithfulness and how He is for us. They believe in us, spurring us on to our destiny. They remind us that we are not alone in this fight. Lastly, they come alongside of us and correct us when we need it. You may not think that you need correcting, but you do, I do, we all do so that as spiritual sons and daughters we can grow up to full maturity in Christ.

Spiritual fathers impart their heart and wisdom so we as sons and daughters are able to go further faster as we stand on their shoulders to build on the foundations they have laid before us. This goes back to the generational blessing chapter. I would have never been able to do what I have done for the Lord in the last fifteen years if not for spiritual fathers embracing me, inviting me to do ministry with them in God's house! Spiritual fathers do not envy their sons and daughters; they want them to excel them in their calling. It is a spiritual father's greatest joy to see them do bigger and better things faster than they did. This is a word to all of us who are spiritual fathers to make sure that we are relating this way with those we are raising up. It really impacted David in his leadership of Israel.

When David was not invited by his natural dad to be considered for the calling of king when Samuel the prophet came to choose Israel's next king, he must have been very wounded by that, perhaps a sense of rejection or feelings of unworthiness? David was a first generation king, and then his leader or perhaps what might be considered his spiritual father, Saul, was intimidated by David's success so he was trying to kill him. I do believe it affected David's life as a father.

There are many people in the ministry who did not know their natural father who would benefit greatly from having a spiritual father. Then some may have been mishandled by their spiritual leader who now are out in ministry struggling today and considering giving up the calling God has on their lives. Ninety percent of people who enter full-time vocation in ministry don't retire from ministry. Could part of the reason be because of a lack of good spiritual fathering in the Body of Christ? I am sure there are many factors for this, but I also believe that good spiritual fathering can help change that.

Others may have a successful ministry like David, but are still struggling to reproduce sons who can flourish for more than one generation. In fact, when you look at the church today, there are many churches that had a great man of God in leadership, but when he passed on, the church died with him. David did well to raise up Solomon, and as the great, wise leader that he was, would that be the goal that David had for him when he passed the baton?

Or what about the tragic story of David and Absalom? David was not fully fathered correctly, and we see that as he did some great things as a father, but no father is perfect by any means. However, when David's daughter was raped by another one of his sons, Amnon, David didn't handle it correctly, which led to Absalom having to take matters into his own hands. Absalom killed Amnon, which broke David's heart.

Absalom then became angry with David, which led to war between father and son. David refused to kill his son, but he had chances to confront his son to try to make things right but never did. He had two years to act on what he knew his heart was telling him to do. Reconcile with his son while he had the chance.

Let me encourage all fathers right here, spiritual and natural, to take that step towards your child if there have been some differences or bitter unforgiveness while you have the chance. It is clearly the work of the enemy to bring division. Satan wants to destroy your children and your legacy, so you and I must humble ourselves when we blow it or if they do and make it right. Don't let the enemy destroy your relationship with your child as he did with David and Absalom.

David finally allowed Absalom to come before him and he kissed him. However, this was short-lived as Absalom felt it was insincere, causing him to be even more furious. Their story ends in tragedy as one of David's men went against David's orders to be gentle with Absalom, and he killed him with three spears through the heart. David was crushed and I am sure full of regrets for not acting when he should have as a father.

Being a father spiritually or naturally is not easy. It takes guts and grace to do it well, but all things are possible through Christ who gives us strength. Fathers, may we learn from David's mistakes, which is the highest form of wisdom, learning from someone else's pain. Dads, may we be quick to repent and say that we messed up. May we be swift to seek forgiveness.

There have been many times when I have had to do that with my natural and spiritual children. I have had to look them in the eye and say. "What I did was wrong. I shouldn't have done that. Please forgive me." I think it models out humility and shows them that we mess up from time to time. It says to them that "even I, as a father, need the grace and mercy of God." It models what repentance looks like so they know how to do it when they need to do so. It also opens the door for them to say, "I am sorry" or "Forgive me too." Remember the father's heart turns first to his child, then the child's heart will turn to him.

David did not do that and his purpose with Absalom went unfulfilled. Absalom didn't finish his assignment. God wants us to finish our assignments for ourselves as well as for our children.

The good news is that God is so graciously turning hearts to Him so that we as fathers can turn to our children's hearts for healing and reconciliation. He is raising up leaders (fathers) who are Kingdom minded, who are blessing their spiritual children to go to their destiny, to go do it big for the Kingdom. God is changing the landscape of our world. It doesn't mean they will always agree, but they will agree to repent, forgive and move forward so that the assignment of the Kingdom can be completed.

God is at work empowering His sons and daughters to finish the assignments He has given them in this world for Him. God wants us to finish strong. People don't always remember how you started, but they do remember how you finish. God wants you to be able to echo Paul when he came to the end of his life and was able to say, *"I have fought the good fight, I have finished the race, and I have remained faithful"* (2 Timothy 4:7). God wants us to finish our race too.

There is something powerful that happens when a father and/or a spiritual father lays his hands on us, looks us in the eye and says, "You are my son. You are my daughter. I am proud of you and pleased with you." There is something even more powerful when we hear God the Father say that through His Word and His Spirit. Remember, the heart of a son or daughter is shaped in the breath of a father.

God knew in advance your need for a father and that is why you need to be validated and accepted as a son or a daughter. This helps us to know who we are and whose we are. Then, you will feel secure in your identity. You can then be comfortable in your own skin, and you can be the original God intended you to be. As author John Mason once said, "You're born an original, don't die a copy!" Fathers are to confirm what God has placed inside of us, speak to our potential and release us to fulfill it.

Now let me be clear. You can have your natural dad be your spiritual father. I know men who have this great blessing in their lives. But for most who have been connected with a spiritual father or fathers, they are not your natural father. The generations are crying out for fathers to take their place and for men to man up! Men, it is time to man up and take our place in this world. Yes, take our stand against the forces of darkness that have been afflicting our sons and daughters for generations! It is a time to take action and do whatever needs to be done to be an active voice in their lives to shape them for their destiny. We need fathers to step up naturally and spiritually. You don't have to be a spiritual father. You can be a mentor, a coach or serve in a local church in student and children's ministries.

MENTORS

Another reality check was a report I heard on the news sometime back, that boys of single moms are staying home longer, struggling to enter manhood, crippled due to the lack of a father assisting in the transition from boys to men. That is one of a father's greatest responsibilities is to help sons transition into manhood. It's not that mothers can't because some have, but most don't because they aren't supposed to. I honestly believe that is why spiritual fathers, father figures and mentors are so needed today in our culture. They can help validate and affirm us and launch us into our purpose in the Kingdom of God.

This is a principle that we see with Jesus and the Father. When Jesus was baptized by John, the Bible says in Mark 1:11 NKJV, *"Then a voice came from heaven, 'You are My beloved Son, in whom I am well pleased.'"* Even Jesus, the Son of God, needed to be validated. He also needed to have the approval of His Father verbally to launch Him into His earthly ministry.

As I said, you don't have to be a spiritual father. You can be a mentor to your kids and to others who don't have a dad. There are ways you can help make a difference in the lives of other children who need you. Great ways include:

- Find out how to join/start All-Pro Dads in your child's school. Visit www.allprodad.com.

- Find out how to join/start Watch D.O.G.S. in your child's school. Visit www.fathers.com.

- Find out how to join/start a biblically based mentoring program. Visit www.christianmentors.org.

My wife and I launched our own called "Dream Builders." We developed a relationship with a willing local school teacher who sponsored us, and we met after school hours on Wednesdays. We would have snacks, do a game and then I or my wife would speak on a specified topic. Other successful people from the community offer their time as well. People like our County Chairman or a local business person speaks.

Students must also spend at least two Saturday mornings serving the community by assisting the Henry Fuller Center to remodel someone's home. At the end of the eleven-week semester, participants are asked to give a power point presentation of what they took away from the training in front of the whole class. Upon successful completion, we give out Bibles and lay our hands on them to pray for and validate them because most of them have never had that before. I can't tell you all of the powerful results we see from this model. Our heart is to train more mentors so we can branch out to other schools.

You can also serve at church, get involved in student and children's ministries. You don't have to know a lot, just be around and serve them by taking the lead. Show them that they matter. It is not just the women who should be involved. At our church, I strongly encourage dads to serve with their wives as a team. I am so blessed to see all the husband-wife couples we have serving so faithfully in our children's and student ministries. You could also launch a small group for dads using this book or others. For more information about our church you can go to www.turningpointchurch.tv.

Another phenomenal idea is to start a Father-Daughter Dance at your church or school.

In 2008, I had an idea for a Father-Daughter Dance at our church. This special night would encourage dads and daughters to intentionally connect. I cast the vision to our small staff and some volunteers. My desire was to create an annual event to foster this very special relationship. I was so grateful to have them buy in and lay out our very first dance. It was small, but we launched it anyway. We had around thirty dads and daughters our first year, around forty-five our second and now, having just completed our third annual dance, we had around one hundred dads and daughters at the event.

It even caught the ear of the local newspaper who made it a headline on the main page. What a thrill it was to see all of those dads and daughters dancing, laughing and deepening their relationships.

As I am wrapping up this chapter, we are actually planning our fifth. We had to cut it off because we ran out of room. Praise God that dads are responding! We are moving into a larger building to allow us to have more dads and daughters come and participate in this dance.

I have now heard of schools and other churches doing the dances, and I celebrate that! I hope every church and school in America and around the world would do one. You can start one. If you want ideas or an outline of what we do, don't hesitate to reach out to our staff. We will gladly give you everything we have, and you can take it and run with it!

You can also coach at a local youth recreation center or event. I have had the joy and hard work of coaching my boys for the last six years in football, baseball and basketball. Yes, it's hard work and it requires good management, but I know that I am not only investing in my boys but in all the youth that I am coaching. We pray and encourage these boys every week, so let's man up! Let's be difference makers and game changers for these children who may not have another positive male role model in their young lives. It is true that there aren't many fathers, but God is changing that with men who are willing and available to step up!

Once you have read this book, begin to live it out and then share it with other men and give it away. You can start a small group for other dads to encourage them to man up. If you want to cause hell to tremble, then step up in the power of our everlasting Father to overthrow the works of darkness in our land. The devil knows that if a person can understand who they are and whose they are, they will be validated. With validation comes confidence and stability. You can be the dad you never had. God believes in you and so do I. Even if you don't come from a strong heritage of fathers, you can be used by God to start one worth passing on. God has a phenomenal legacy for you, my friend. It is time to believe that and live like that. You can do it! You can make it! Don't quit, no matter what!

Got Father?

Do you remember the story of Jason Davis, famous billionaire grandson of Marvin Davis I mentioned earlier? Let me repeat it again with a little more insight to encourage you. Jason was in a counseling session on "Celebrity Rehab with Dr. Drew." On one particular show where Jason was in a counseling session to try and figure out where the addictive behavior stemmed from, he found it was the fact that Jason had access to all the money he could ever want, but didn't have access to the thing he needed the most – the love of his father.

Jason stated in the session that what he wanted was a father to turn to. Dr. Drew told him that he didn't get to have that. To see his countenance drop was something that I could totally identify with and my heart hurt for him, because I truly understood his pain. I understood where Dr. Drew was coming from, but the truth is, he can have that, and it can come through having a spiritual father or mentor, a father figure in his life.

I needed that in a big way because I didn't have that, but because of God's amazing grace, I got that and still need it. It continues to have a profound effect in my stability. And, yes, we who don't have that father to turn to need to be assured that we can have that. You can have a father or a father figure to turn to for affirmation, direction and comfort. Spiritual fathers come alongside us to comfort us and they even correct us when necessary.

Pray to the heavenly Father and seek Him for a godly father figure. One of my spiritual fathers says, "When the student is ready, the teacher will appear." So I would say, "When the son or daughter is ready, the father will appear."

Don't be ashamed that you don't have a father figure in your life right now, and don't feel weak because you acknowledge that you need one if you want one. You and I were wired that way by our heavenly Father. God affirmed Jesus and said He was well pleased with Him, and today God wants to validate His children and see them restored.

Again, we must learn to be sons and daughters first so that we can be good mothers and fathers. God wants to validate you, so you can be forgiven, healed, affirmed and launched into your life purpose. God wants to validate you today. If you need Him to validate you, just ask and receive from Him.

God is restoring fathers to the Body, because He is raising sons and daughters to build the Kingdom for His imminent return. You are a part of God's plan to change things. God is preparing you for what He has assigned you to do. Each of us can make a difference and change the world, one life at a time. This generation is crying out for change, and you are the change they are waiting for. So activate your faith and just do it!

CHAPTER 12

Daddy's Watching

I REMEMBER A cool November night in the fall of 1983 when the eighth grade football Morrow Bobcats were playing in the county semifinals. I was so stoked to play under the lights at the high school stadium as hundreds would be in attendance at that night's game.

The band was playing and the people were streaming into the stands. However, I was extremely aware of the rarity that my father was going to be in the stands watching me play that night. There were several hundred in attendance that night, but in my mind, there was only one person in the midst of the multitudes that I was playing for. I was playing for an audience of one, my dad. There was just something inside of me that caused me to play at my highest level that night. It was like my goal was to be in on every play of the game so that my dad would hear my name called out on the loud speaker to make him proud to be my dad.

I truly had the game of my life. Two solo sacks, numerous tackles and a tipped away pass that would have been a potential touchdown for the opposing team. When the game was over, guess who I was searching for to be congratulated by? That's right, my dad! I had played for an audience of one.

Now even as a grown man, father, husband and pastor in full-time ministry, I find fulfillment in sharing what God is doing in and through me with my biological father, stepfather and my spiritual fathers. I find that I can somehow show them that their love and time have made a difference in my life. I am still growing, still learning and still needing to lean on them, learn from them and celebrate with them. It still brings me great joy to be able to speak with each of them.

In life and in ministry, we can battle loneliness, but I have found with these fathers and my heavenly Father, I am not alone, even if the enemy tries to convince me that I am. Neither are you, my friend. You have the eyes of the Father watching you day and night. His thoughts toward you are as numerous as the sand on the seashore.

Psalm 139:17,18 says, *"How precious are your thoughts about me, O God. They cannot be numbered! I can't even count them; they outnumber the grains of sand!"*

Think about that! God's thoughts of you are more than all the single grains of sand upon the entire earth, including the beaches and deserts. You are on His mind constantly. You may not be focused on Him, but never forget that He is totally focused on you when you get up and when you lie down. Wherever you go, wherever you could go and wherever you are today, He is watching you. We all need to know this timeless truth, and we need to be reminded that we are the apple of His eye.

Like any good father, He loves to watch us, even when we make mistakes. He is a patient Dad who will gently teach us the right way, and He will never leave us or give up on us.

Even now as a follower of Jesus Christ, when I feel discouraged or feel that no one sees what I do for the Kingdom or what I am becoming, I remember the truth that my heavenly Father is in the grandstands of heaven watching my every move, my every play. I am the apple of His eye, and His thoughts toward me are more numerous than all the sand on the earth. My Daddy is always watching and every day I am playing for an audience of one. That's my sincere prayer for all of us, that we would approach every day with this comfort and attitude of giving it our all, our very best because we know it will not go unnoticed. We can live by faith loving God, loving people and serving the world because we know that He will reward us according to our actions. He will not forget us, and He will always be watching.

NIGHT OF HOPE

On Friday, March 18, 2011, I was able attend Joel and Victoria Osteen's Night of Hope in Nashville, Tennessee. Again, I was deeply impacted by this event and am every time I have the opportunity to experience the legacy of fifty-two years of family ministry that have come from John Osteen.

My favorite part of the night was when Joel was sharing a message about being surrounded by such a great cloud of witnesses of faith in the grandstands of heaven. He spoke about Rahab, Job and others. The last person's story he talked about was a seventeen-year-old popcorn salesman with no education, no family lineage or money. He burst into tears and had to bury his face into his hands in front of 16,000 people. Even after being gone for twelve years, he was referring to his daddy – John Osteen.

It was such a God moment for me when I think about how powerful an impact a father can have on his children and the world for good even after he has left this planet. I couldn't imagine what that must have felt like as a son, because I don't have that in my life. However, I knew I wanted to experience it as a father. I want to have that kind of impact on my boys and my daughter long after I am gone from this world.

This session ended with Joel quoting his daddy's favorite poem.

He started the first line and then big as life was a jumbo screen directly behind Joel with his father walking and finishing the poem while looking directly at the camera. In that moment, I could see that Joel knew and could boldly say, "My heavenly Daddy and my biological daddy are still watching me! He is still alive and they are now together watching me, cheering for me and celebrating me from heaven."

Who's Your Daddy?

Maybe you have read this book and you don't have a father in your life. You don't know what the love of a father is like. You know it's something you want. It's something you are open to, but you feel all alone in this world. I know exactly how you feel. I was there. It's a very lonely place. But the good news is, you don't have to feel alone for another second of another day. If God hasn't made it clear from the previous chapters of this book that He is reaching out specifically to you and you are still wondering if there is real hope of God desiring you, let me make it crystal clear.

How do you become a child of God? Jesus gives us the answer in the Gospel of Mark, chapter 10, verses 13-15: *"One day some parents brought their children to Jesus so he could touch and bless them. But the disciples scolded the parents for bothering him. When Jesus saw what was happening, he was angry with his disciples. He said to them, 'Let the children come to me. Don't stop them! For the Kingdom of God belongs to those who are like these children. I tell you the truth, anyone who doesn't receive the Kingdom of God like a child will never enter it.'"*

The reference to being a child is very comforting to me. Children come humbly without reservations. They come with openness and faith. We don't have to have it all together or be without fault. We simply come as we are with childlike faith, and He will receive us. He will be a Father to us.

God wants you to know that He is watching and He is here for you. He wants you. He wanted you before you even got your name. It is the heart of the good news of Jesus Christ. God wanted a family, so He sent His only Son Jesus Christ to die for us. God wants to be your Father. He is a Father to the fatherless and places the lonely in families. He sets the prisoners free and gives them joy (Psalm 68:5,6).

God wants to set you free from your past sins, failures, loneliness and anything else that has held you back from becoming who it is that He has called you to be. He has called you to be a son or a daughter of promise. He has called you to be a son or a daughter of purpose. He sets the prisoners free and places them in families. God wants to set you free, place you in His family, the Body of Christ, the Kingdom of God, the Church. God wants to give you a spiritual family in a local church so that you can get planted and flourish in His house (Psalm 92:13). You can become His son or daughter if you haven't already by calling upon the name of Jesus.

John 1:12,13 says, *"But to all who believed him and accepted him, he gave the right to become children of God. They are reborn – not with a physical birth resulting from human passion or plan, but a birth that comes from God."*

If you will accept and believe on the only begotten Son of the Father, Jesus, you can become His child. You can be born again. That is God's desire for you. He wanted you as His child, so He sent His Son to die for you and take your place at the judgment of the cross. God is not mad at you; He is madly in love with you! So accept the facts. God loves you unconditionally and consistently. He doesn't love you randomly or based upon your performance. He loves you with an everlasting, eternal, unfailing love. You just have to believe it and accept it.

Dealing with Your BS – Belief System

Speaking of believing, I would like to leave you with a final thought as we close this book. I want to make sure I leave you with a powerful truth that has helped me tremendously. The thought is about your heart and how you see yourself.

God wants to heal your heart and He actually wants to give you a new heart. When you are born again, you receive a new heart. Read what God said He would do in Ezekiel 11:19,20:

And I will give them singleness of heart and put a new spirit within them. I will take away their stony, stubborn heart and give them a tender, responsive heart, so they will obey my decrees and regulations. Then they will truly be my people, and I will be their God.

God gives you a new heart and He wants you to see yourself as He does. I have noticed that even for those who become a child of God, we can struggle with not seeing ourselves as God does. God sees us as His children. He believes in us, He believes in you. Therefore, you should believe in you. We have to deal with our belief system or the picture we see of ourselves.

God wants us to live like sons and daughters. He wants us to live as we are — loved, chosen, strong, gifted, favored and victorious. If you don't see yourself as God does, you can never be what He has called you to be. What picture do you see of yourself? Do you see yourself defeated, never being able to forgive someone and move on? Do you see yourself never succeeding because you don't get the right breaks or know the right people? Or do you see yourself growing in wisdom and favor with God and with man? Do you see yourself rising above your circumstances as the overcomer God called you to be?

The picture you see on the inside of your heart, your belief system, is directly connected to the way you will experience life. Until I knew I was loved, forgiven, chosen and appointed by God, I didn't believe in myself. I was living defeated as a victim far from God and far from hope. I didn't realize all God had planned for me as a son in His family. I could never have dreamed God had these amazing plans for me and that He already placed everything I needed to fulfill His plan for my life on the inside of me. You have to see yourself the same way.

God chose you and designed you for greatness. You can't believe in the greatness of God without believing about the greatness within you. Greater is He that is in you, than he that is in the world (1 John 4:4). The way you think about yourself and the way you see yourself are directly connected to the quality of life you will experience as a son or daughter of God. Remember what the Bible says about this: *"For as he thinks in his heart, so is he"* (Proverbs 23:7 NKJV).

You may feel like where you are is not where you want to be, but if you will get your belief system in sync with God's in regard to who you really are as a child of God, you will succeed in life. If you will see it in your heart, you will see it in your life. It reminds me of another story I read about recently concerning a beggar and a banker.

There was a banker who always tossed a coin in the cup of a legless beggar who sat on the street outside of the bank. But, unlike most people, the banker would always insist on getting one of the pencils the man had beside him. "You are a merchant," the banker would say, "and I always expect to receive good value from the merchants I do business with."

One day the legless man was not on the sidewalk. Time passed and the banker forgot about him, until he walked into a public building and there in the concession stand sat the former beggar. He was obviously the owner of his own small business now.

"I have always hoped you would come by someday," the man said. "You are largely responsible for me being here. You kept telling me that I was a 'merchant.' *I started thinking of myself that way,* instead of a beggar receiving gifts. I started selling pencils – lots of them. You gave me self-respect, caused me to look at myself differently."

The difference was someone saw him different, and it helped him to believe it himself. It caused him to rise above his disability and reach his potential. That beggar represents you and me. God the Father represents the banker as He has not just rescued us, but He has believed in us even when we were down. He speaks life and potential to us again and again until we can start to see ourselves as sons and daughters of the Almighty God, the everlasting Father. It is when we believe what He says about us that we too overcome every obstacle, rise up and take our place in His Kingdom. We begin to live a life of purpose with every step. We live a life that loves to bring Him glory. This is the place that He is most glorified and we are most satisfied.

Dream big about what God can do through your life. When you do, just know that you are dreaming like your Father who is the biggest dreamer! He has a dream for your life. He wants you blessed, prospering, healthy, thriving and living in abundance. You don't have to sit at the back of the bus anymore, because your Daddy owns the bus line.

Catch the vision and write it down for your life, your family and children. Think big and know that if you can see the invisible, you can do the impossible. Don't let your belief system stop you from fulfilling your potential.

Don't get stuck in a rut of your past. You may have had failures. We all have. You can get up again. You can believe that your best days are still in front of you and closer than you think. Get God's promises on the inside of you as His son, His daughter. Get that picture of yourself that He has given you of access to His Kingdom. In fact, He said it is His pleasure to give you His Kingdom. Begin to see yourself winning in life and in relationships and develop the belief system your God wants for you. You will fulfill God's will for your life in your generation and in the generations to come!

As a son or a daughter, you need to always remind yourself when you feel all alone that He is watching you. He knows your every thought, your every move, your every fear, concern and victory. He will never leave you or forsake you. He will NEVER leave you orphaned or abandoned. He loves watching you, and even if you fall, He will be there to pick you up again and again. He is there with you every step of the way, cheering you on, calling out your name, saying, "That's My boy, that's My girl, and I am well pleased with them."

I found a letter put together that I have used several times in one of the services I have ministered at as a student pastor and as a lead pastor. It is called "The Father's Love Letter." It is a very powerful biblical letter laid out as a love letter straight from God's Word to you personally.

Yes, it is to us all whom He loves, but I want you to read it as if God were speaking it directly to you. That's what I love about Father God is that He is personal. Jesus is personal. I love the way He makes me feel like His favorite child. He doesn't show partiality, but He can make you feel like you are His favorite.

I wanted to end this book and chapter by sharing this powerful letter from God, your eternal Father, to you. Check out the Father's love letter to you!

My Child...

You may not know Me, but I know everything about you.
Psalm 139:1

I know when you sit down and when you rise up.
Psalm 139:2

I am familiar with all your ways. Psalm 139:3

Even the very hairs on your head are numbered.
Matthew 10:29-31

For you were made in My image. Genesis 1:27

In Me you live and move and have your being. Acts 17:28

For you are My offspring. Acts 17:28

I knew you even before you were conceived. Jeremiah 1:4,5

I chose you when I planned creation. Ephesians 1:11,12

You were not a mistake, for all your days are written
in My book. Psalm 139:15,16

I determined the exact time of your birth and where you would live. Acts 17:26

You are fearfully and wonderfully made. Psalm 139:14

I knit you together in your mother's womb. Psalm 139:13

And brought you forth on the day you were born. Psalm 71:6

I have been misrepresented by those who don't know Me. John 8:41-44

I am not distant and angry, but am the complete expression of love. 1 John 4:16

And it is My desire to lavish My love on you. 1 John 3:1

Simply because you are My child and I am your Father. 1 John 3:1

I offer you more than your earthly father ever could. Matthew 7:11

For I am the perfect Father. Matthew 5:48

Every good gift that you receive comes from My hand. James 1:17

For I am your provider and I meet all your needs. Matthew 6:31-33

My plan for your future has always been filled with hope. Jeremiah 29:11

Because I love you with an everlasting love. Jeremiah 31:3

My thoughts toward you are countless as the sand on
the seashore. Psalms 139:17,18

And I rejoice over you with singing. Zephaniah 3:17

I will never stop doing good to you. Jeremiah 32:40

For you are My treasured possession. Exodus 19:5

I desire to establish you with all my heart and all my soul.
Jeremiah 32:41

And I want to show you great and marvelous things.
Jeremiah 33:3

If you seek Me with all your heart, you will find Me.
Deuteronomy 4:29

Delight in Me and I will give you the desires of your heart.
Psalm 37:4

For it is I who gave you those desires. Philippians 2:13

I am able to do more for you than you could possibly imagine.
Ephesians 3:20

For I am your greatest encourager. 2 Thessalonians 2:16,17

I am also the Father who comforts you in all your troubles.
2 Corinthians 1:3,4

When you are brokenhearted, I am close to you. Psalm 34:18

As a shepherd carries a lamb, I have carried you close
to My heart. Isaiah 40:11

One day I will wipe away every tear from your eyes.
Revelation 21:3,4

And I'll take away all the pain you have suffered on
this earth. Revelation 21:3,4

I am your Father, and I love you even as I love
My Son, Jesus. John 17:23

For in Jesus, My love for you is revealed. John 17:26

He is the exact representation of My being. Hebrews 1:3

He came to demonstrate that I am for you, not against you.
Romans 8:31

And to tell you that I am not counting your sins.
2 Corinthians 5:18,19

Jesus died so that you and I could be reconciled.
2 Corinthians 5:18,19

His death was the ultimate expression of My love for you.
1 John 4:10

I gave up everything I loved that I might gain your love.
Romans 8:31,32

If you receive the gift of My Son Jesus, you receive Me.
1 John 2:23

And nothing will ever separate you from
My love again. Romans 8:38,39

Come home and I'll throw the biggest party heaven
has ever seen. Luke 15:7

I have always been Father and will always be Father.
Ephesians 3:14,15

My question is … Will you be My child? John 1:12,13

I am waiting for you. Luke 15:11-32

Love, Your Dad
Almighty God

Father's Love Letter used by permission Father Heart Communications
© 1999-2011 www.FathersLoveLetter.com

Conclusion

As WE COME to the end of this book, I pray that it is the beginning of a turning point for you. A turning point is defined as: *a point at which significant change occurs.* My prayer and hope is that this would mark significant change for you. We all want to change our lives for the good. Many times in life we may have regrets and feel like we fall short. Maybe you do have regrets; maybe you have made some mistakes. We all have. One thing I know is that we can feel unfulfilled and unsatisfied with our lives. The truth is that more stuff, more things and more of what the world has to offer will never fill that void. Only God can fill that void and what's really important at the end of our lives is relationships, our relationship with Jesus Christ, our family, and our children. Having been in ministry now for over seventeen years I have been with people at their time of death. When people are dying they don't ask for more time at the office nor do they ask for a snapshot of their portfolio. They don't say, "Can I go to the bank one more time?" and "Boy, I wish I would have worked more or spent more time alone." No, they ask for those they love and care about the most. We have the chance now to make things right, to step towards God, to step towards forgiveness, healing and restoration. This is your chance to take steps towards that significant change. Time is the most precious commodity that we have and we only have a limited amount of it.

So let's pray like Moses in Psalm 90:12 NIV, *"Teach us to number our days aright, that we may gain a heart of wisdom."* Perhaps we have been wounded, abandoned and done wrong. It may have hardened our hearts and caused us to be stubborn. Haven't we spent enough time making foolish decisions and allowing pride to keep us from God and from those we really love? But now may we have a humble teachable heart and make wise decisions. We can use the rest of our time on this earth, whether it's five years or fifty, loving God and loving our family. I can tell you that it's time well spent and it's a wise investment when we do. It not only benefits us in this life, but in the one to come, as well as in the lives of those coming after us. One right decision can change a lifetime of mistakes. So do it now while you have the chance, don't wait for it to come to you, make your move, seize your divine moment right now.

FATHERS

Maybe you have blown it. Maybe you have made mistakes. Big mistakes. Guess what, we all have. There are no perfect dads. There is only one perfect Father and that is God. As you look to Him for strength and walk in His love, you can be the Dad you have always wanted and wanted to be. Whether you are a married father or a single father, remember that your children love you forever. There is no one that can take your place. From the time we come out of the womb we look for you, your voice, your touch and your love. We need it. Give it as best you can and as much as you can. Will you fight for your children? Will you be there for them, no matter what?

If there has been strife and separation, will you turn your heart towards your children regardless of what they have done or said? If they have hardened their heart towards you or won't speak to you, go after them at any cost. They want you too. Even when they say they don't. If you will genuinely love them and reach out to them and remember God's love never fails. It never quits and never gives up. Your love can change them forever, so be confident and go for it. Take the initiative, take the first step, one step at a time, one foot in front of the other. You are the leader so lead well. It's not how you start that people remember, it's how you finish. So don't ever quit, Dad, no matter how hard it gets or how much it costs. Pay the price to be the pioneer that will initiate the generational blessings of God for you, your children and your children's children.

SONS AND DAUGHTERS

As a son who went through divorce and fatherlessness, but also as a faithful father, I know both sides of these lives. I can tell you that it may be hard to forgive because you hurt so deep and so bad, but you can let go now. It's going to be all right. God has this in His grip. He loves you and nothing you can ever do can separate you from the Father's love. You don't have to be afraid of being abandoned. You don't have to feel alone or unwanted anymore. It's not your fault because of what happened. You were not the problem, sin was. Your father is not your enemy. Satan is. I pray that you can look through the lens of grace as I did to extend that forgiveness to your father, not because he deserves it, but because he needs it. If there is time and opportunity for reconciliation and restoration, then please let it begin. Don't allow it to rob you of your peace and fulfillment for one more second. Have hope, because our God is turning this thing around and you can learn from this pain to be the father, the mother that God has purposed you to be. The curse can be reversed into blessing. God wants to and can change your family tree through you. What the devil meant for evil God can turn it into good. Until you confront and deal with this wound from your father, you can never truly be fruitful and fulfill God's perfect will for your life. If you allow God, He can not only heal you, your father and your children, but he can heal others who are all around you dealing with the same thing as you.

I pray that you will know from this day forward who you are and Whose you are. I pray that you will live like a son/daughter of promise and take your place in the Father's Kingdom fulfilling your purpose in Him! Let nothing stop you now. Go forward to your destiny. May your children go further faster than you as you pass to them a heritage of healing that will be a legacy that outlives you in the generations to come. It could be that in the years to come your great grandchildren will talk about your life of faith and how you changed their world by humbling yourself before God to allow His blessing to flow to them. All things are possible to him who believes!

SINGLE MOMS

I salute you. You inspire us so deeply. Though you may often feel invisible and underappreciated, your sacrifices seemingly unnoticed day after day, I am telling you this, one day your children will rise up and call you blessed. Live a life of faith to the fullest. Continue to model Christ to your children. Give them your love, strength and character. Lead by example and stick to your convictions. Don't let guilt cause you to compromise. Hold true to your word and don't make empty threats. Your children have had enough to walk through in divorce or living without Dad, to not trust what you say. Do what you say, even if it's hard and if it hurts. They want you to. Love them and discipline them in the ways approved by the Lord. If it weren't for you, what would happen to them? May God continue to give you grace and supply all your needs according to His riches in glory.

Some of you may have the blessing of a Dad who is involved so thank God for that! Some of you do not, so don't lose your hope or your mind. God is faithful and He will give you what He promised as you continue to live by faith. You are so very important, so very appreciated and so very vital to what God is doing in our world! Don't give up and remember that at the end of your life, when you think no one else noticed… God did and He will reward you according to your deeds. Keep on keeping on. The best is still yet to come!

Let the turning begin and the blessing flow once again until He comes.

NOTES

Chapter 2

[1] National Center for Fathering, Fathering in America Poll, January 1999.

[2] U.S. Census Bureau, Children's Living Arrangements and Characteristics: March 2002, P20-547, Table C8. Washington, DC: GPO 2003. "One in Four: America's Youngest Poor." National Center for Children in Poverty, 1996.

[3] U.S. Department of Health and Human Services. National Center for Health Statistics. Survey on Child Health. Washington, DC, 1993. Denton, Rhonda E. and Charlene M. Kampfe. "The Relationship Between Family Variables and Adolescent Substance Abuse: A Literature Review." Adolescence 114 (1994): 475-495.

[4] U.S. Department of Health and Human Services. Public Health Service. Center for Disease Control and Prevention. National Center for Health Statistics. Report to Congress on Out-of-Wedlock Childbearing. Hyattsville, MD (Sept. 1995): 12. Hong, Gong-Soog and Shelly L. White-Means. "Do Working Mothers Have Healthy Children?" Journal of Family and Economic Issues 14 (Summer 1993): 163-186. Stanton, U.S. Department of Health and Human Services. National Center for Health Statistics. "National Health Interview Survey." Hyattsville, MD, 1988. Elshtain, Jean Bethke. "Family Matters: The Plight of America's Children." The Christian Century (July 1993): 14-21.

[5] McLanahan, Sara and Gary Sandefur. Growing up with a Single Parent: What Hurts, What Helps. Cambridge: Harvard University Press, 1994. U.S. Department of Health and Human Services.

National Center for Health Statistics. Survey on Child Health. Washington, DC; GPO, 1993. One-Parent Families and Their Children: The School's Most Significant Minority. The Consortium for the Study of School Needs of Children from One-Parent Families. National Association of Elementary School Principals and the Institute for Development of Educational Activities, a division of the Charles F. Kettering Foundation. Arlington, VA 1980.

6 "Life Without Father," copyright 1996 by David Popenoe. Reprinted by permission of the Free Press, an imprint of Simon & Schuster, Inc. Center for Disease Control. U.S. Department of Health and Human Services. National Center for Health Statistics. National Health Interview Survey. Hyattsville, MD, 1988: Heimer, Karen. "Gender, Interaction, and Delinquency: Testing a Theory of Differential Social Control." Social Psychology Quarterly 59 (1996): 39-61.: Conseur, Amy et al. "Maternal and Perinatal Risk Factors for Later Delinquency." Pediatrics 99 (1997): 785-790.

7 Billy, John O. G., Karin L. Brewster and William R. Grady. "Contextual Effects on the Sexual Behavior of Adolescent Women." Journal of Marriage and Family 56 (1994): Survey. Hyattsville, MD 1988.Whitehead, Barbara Dafoe. "Facing the Challenges of Fragmented Families." The Philanthropy Roundtable 9.1 (1995): 21.

AUTHOR CONTACT INFORMATION

To purchase books, for more information, or to schedule Michael Turner to speak, please contact:

Michael Turner

info@watchmedaddybook.com

770.898.5277

www.watchmedaddybook.com

www.turningpointchurch.tv

NOTES

NOTES

NOTES

NOTES